RAF TRAINERS
Volume 1 - 1918-1945

Written and Illustrated by Peter Freeman
with Tim Walsh

Series Editor Neil Robinson

First published in the UK in 2012 by

AIRfile Publications Ltd
Hoyle Mill
Barnsley
South Yorkshire S71 1HN

Compiled by Neil Robinson
AIRgen Publications

Illustrations Copyright Peter Freeman 2012

ISBN 978-0-9569802-4-3

Design: Mark Hutchinson

Printed in the UK by
PHP Litho Printers Ltd
Hoyle Mill
Barnsley
South Yorkshire S71 1HN

Acknowledgments
Our warmest thanks go to all the people who have contributed in the production of this book. Special thanks must go to Mike Starmer for his endless supply of reference material and all things military. Also to Jon Freeman who has supported us with drawing research and reference. While recognising that specific works on RAF training are few and far between, we must highlight the contribution of Ray Sturtivant's publications, 'RAF Flying Training and Support Units since 1912' (Air Britain (Historians) Ltd 2007) and 'The History of Britain's Military Training Aircraft' (Ray Sturtivant and Haynes Publishing Group 1987) and 'By the Seat of Your Pants: Basic Training of Royal Air Force Pilots in Rhodesia, Canada, South Africa and U.S.A. During World War 2' by Hugh Morgan (Newton Publishers 1990).

Peter Freeman & Tim Walsh

AIRfile
to inform and inspire

A range of illustrated camouflage and markings guides, full of well-researched, clear and unambiguous full colour illustrations, with detailed informative captions, produced by a cooperative of well-known aviation enthusiasts, authors and illustrators, designed to provide comprehensive camouflage scheme and markings coverage, culled from a variety of areas including previously published material, official and private documents and photo collections, and primary sources.

Used either as a one-stop reference source, or as an integral part of your research in to the fascinating study of colour schemes and markings carried by combat aircraft from World War One to the present day, each AIRfile aims to show the chronology and development of the schemes and markings of the aircraft in question, including the many anomalies and inevitable misinterpretations and errors occasionally to be found on operational military aircraft.

RAF Trainers
Volume 1 - 1918-1945

Whilst there have been inumerable books published on the history of the RAF and the wars that it fought in up to 1945, there has been little produced on the training of its aircrew. Equally, this period has been well documented both, photographically and illustratively, but these, by and large, concentrate on the front line aircraft.

The purpose of this book is to show the wide range of not only aircraft that were used in the training role, but also the colour schemes that abounded, especially at the beginning of the existence of the RAF. The garish and wild colour schemes seen immediately after the Great War were, perhaps, an indication of the great sense of relief to be free of war. Another reason could be the high visibility aspect, as some of these aircraft were flown by experienced instructor pilots at the Flying Schools, maybe an early form of warning to let the student pilots know who the occupant was and to be aware. This impropriety was quickly curtailed by the higher powers (although never completely eradicated) and whilst there was a short period when dark camouflage colours continued, silver dope soon found favour from the early 1920s. Once this colour was applied to the fabric on aircraft, it was found to be a good weatherproof covering, with the added bonus of reflecting the suns rays, a necessity in the hot and sunny areas like Egypt and similar places.

Silver dope was used for a decade, until the early 1930s, when trials took place with yellow dope as a training scheme, and the success of these trials meant that yellow was adopted as a standard overall colour for training aircraft by 1936. With the outbreak of war looking ever more likely, all aircraft began to appear with drab camouflage colours, the fighters and bombers losing their Squadron regalia and silver dope under Dark Green and Dark Earth paint. The upper surfaces of trainers also began to be painted in these new colours, but retained yellow for the undersides, and for a while, to the fuselage sides. Biplanes had a slight variation in the upper colours, a shadow compensating scheme, whereby the upper surfaces of the lower wings were painted instead with Light Earth and Light Green, in the usual disruptive pattern. Wartime conditions would always mean that there would have to be a compromise between camouflage for concealment, and yellow for high visibility. Target tugs had black stripes added to the yellow to show their specialist role, and the Beam Approach Training Flights were adorned with large yellow triangles on the fuselage and wings. There was no such compromise or restriction to trainer aircraft flying in Canada or South Africa. Trainer Yellow was the specified colour and was used in these places without the need of any camouflage colours. Even aircraft that had been sent abroad with the Dark Earth and Dark Green still intact were soon to receive large swathes of yellow on the fuselages and flying surfaces. On their return to British soil, aircrews were sent to the various OTUs and OCUs before going to active Squadrons, and these aircraft were, obviously, in the appropriate camouflage schemes.

This book also illustrates the wide range of aircraft that were eventually called upon to provide training in one form or another, especially during World War Two. While the use of primary training aircraft is obvious, front line bombers and fighters were all employed by the various training schools to provide a more realistic experience for the crews.

In referencing the colours and markings of the aircraft, each illustration has had a photograph as the source material, and the majority of these have obviously been black and white, with all the associated problems that come with trying to interpret the colours, and we hope our best guesses are close. Also, not every training aircraft used by the RAF has been included, as some types were used in only small numbers, and we have tried to stay with the types that were well used – although we have included a few one-offs.

Whether you are an aviation enthusiast, aircraft modeller or just plain interested, we hope you enjoy reading and using this book. We believe it provides a good representation of Training Aircraft in the Royal Air Force from the small beginnings of 1918, up to the end of the World War Two.

Peter Freeman and Tim Walsh, May 2012

The Wright Brothers, Bleriot, Santos-Dumont, A V Roe, Horatio Phillips, Jacob Ellehammer, Farman – all of these aviation pioneers and many more, took their lives into their hands when they made the first tentative hops into the air. That they survived to repeat the feat of flying was more down to luck than to skill or judgement. These first pilots were flying literally 'by the seats of their pants'. They had no-one to show them what to do, to tell them what effects and forces were in play as the fragile stick and string constructions in which they were entrusting their lives staggered airward. Inevitably, there were fatalities. In the decade after the Wright Flyer, some of these early pilots pushed their luck a little too far. Some of these pilots are now little known, for example, the first pilot to be killed by an aeroplane was a Frenchman by the name of Eugene Lefebvre, a most dubious honour, whilst other names would be recognisable today, such as the Hon. C.S. Rolls, the first British pilot to die, and Samuel Cody, an American that did much to bring the world of aviation to the masses, and who lost his life in one of his own designs, near to a place called Farnborough. Even at this early juncture, there were those with the foresight to realise that some kind of training regimen was needed. One of those people was a young man by the name of Thomas Sopwith, who set up his own flying school in 1912, and subsequently trained pilots who would go on to have a great influence in the world of aviation, Harry Hawker and Hugh Trenchard to name but two.

Official interest during these early years was minimal, lacklustre and sometimes completely non-existent. This was to change when it emerged that Britain, and specifically its Armed Forces, were seriously lagging behind the likes of Germany and France, the latter country having to hand some 200 aircraft and over 260 pilots to fly them in 1911. Britain by comparison could only muster a paltry eight aircraft (assuming none of them were broken) and a magnificent total of nineteen pilots. For once, the Government acted with commendable speed, and the committee set up to look into aviation requirements recommended that all the disparate units that existed in the Army and the Navy be brought together to form a Flying Corps. This was approved and acted upon by the Government with a White Paper in April of 1912. One part of this new Flying Corps was to become the Central Flying School based at Upavon. A Royal Warrant was written to allow this new fighting force to be known as the Royal Flying Corps.

The role of the Central Flying School was to train Instructor Pilots, and these pilots would then go on to train the combat pilots that would soon be fighting in the skies over France. The numbers of these pilots would increase as the RFC expanded. The size of the RFC as it flew across the English Channel into battle amounted to a mere four Squadrons of the Expeditionary Force, a grand total of sixty three aircraft and just over 100 men. By the end of hostilities in 1918, this small nucleus had grown into the greatest air force in the world, numbering over 130 Squadrons and over a dozen Flights in France and abroad, with another fifety five Squadrons defending home soil. The Training Squadrons themselves numbered seventy five, while personnel of all ranks were close to 300,000 in service and the number of aircraft had risen to more than 22,500 with the establishment of the Royal Air Force, on 1 April 1918.

The beginning of the Great War had seen the role of the aeroplane as merely a reconnaissance platform, the ability to look over the horizon was useful in planning the strategies of the battles on the ground. However, other uses for this new technology would soon manifest themselves. As more aircraft from both sides began to meet each other in the skies over the battlefields, it was only a matter of time before pilots started to arm themselves with pistols and rifles and started taking pot-shots at each other. The aeroplane began to be seen as capable of carrying bombs, as engine technology moved forward, as a kind of long range artillery.

As is always the case when armed conflict arises, the progress of technology is compressed to a greater degree than it would be in peacetime. Soon there were dedicated aircraft, specific to their intended roles, so the end of the War revealed the aeroplane as fighter, bomber, reconnaissance, torpedo bomber; in its various forms, it had proved itself to be an all round effective weapon.

All of these various aspects of the air war required pilots, navigators, bomb aimers, gunners, riggers, mechanics, et al, to be trained, and to a high degree of competence. As previously mentioned, the Training Depot Stations, Training Squadrons, Flights, Schools and others had increased in number to accommodate all the requirements that the new RAF needed, and is indicative of how diverse the training had become, and how large and far reaching the RAF was. This was not to last.

The period immediately after the end of the Great War was a dangerous time for the RAF, as both the Navy and the Army wanted this new fighting force to be disbanded, with each wanting to take back large portions into their own domains. The only reason that it survived was because the new Secretary for War and Air, Winston Churchill, and his appointing of Hugh Trenchard as Chief of Air Staff, fought for the RAF to be kept as an independent fighting force. Even so, the RAF suffered a 90% reduction in the numbers of men and machines through demobilisation and the need of the Government to try and save money, as the War had cost the country greatly, not only in money, but also in the number of men who were never to return.

Trenchard, hampered though he was by these circumstances, nevertheless laid down the basis of the RAF almost single handedly, including the RAF College at Cranwell in 1920, an Apprentices School at Halton in the same year, and the University Air Squadrons and the Auxiliary Air Force in 1925. Also formed in the immediate Post War years were six Flying Training Squadrons, not to mention the myriad other training units and schools that were created during this period. Trenchard also set out to prove to the politicians that the RAF was a cost effective fighting force, especially overseas. When there were uprisings in the Middle East, the RAF was able to quell them quickly and efficiently, with a minimal loss of life. A similar operation carried out by the Army had been costly in both expense and lives and had taken quite a while to bring it to a conclusion. The RAF began to undertake more of these policing operations during the 1920's and early 1930s, in Africa, the Middle East, and the Far East, many of these operations being very long distance, which eventually layed the foundations for later civil routes.

The 1930s saw a massive expansion programme for the RAF due to events happening on the Continent. Unfortunately, practically all of the aircraft flying with the RAF at this point were obsolescent biplanes, apart from research aircraft and the High Speed Flight, which was taking part in the Schneider Trophy races. For once, Trenchard missed the importance of this contest, considering it of little value. Given that monoplanes were beginning to appear on the Continent and in Russia, completely out-classing RAF types, the aircraft flying in the Schneider

Trophy gave the RAF and the aircraft industry valuable data on monoplanes that would very soon be of paramount importance.

Whilst the RAF had flown around the world, civilian flying had also expanded, the public in general continuing to be fascinated by aviation. Record breaking flights by both civilian and Service pilots made sure that flying schools had a regular business. These civilian schools went through a sea-change when it was decided in 1935 that they would henceforth be responsible for the initial training of pupil pilots for the RAF, leaving the FTS units free to concentrate on more advanced training. The civilian schools were re-named Elementary and Reserve Flying Training Schools, and the initial four were joined in 1939 by another fifty-five. 1936 saw a major re-organisation of the Home Defence Force that had been established back in 1917. This was split into four separate commands, namely Bomber Command, Coastal Command, Fighter Command and Training Command.

By now, many people had realised that war was coming, and the RAF expansion programme, although slow to start initially, began to gather pace. New aircraft types coming into service with the newly created Commands were obviously widely differing in their functions, and in 1937 the Central Flying School was given the task of compiling Pilots Notes for all aircraft coming into the Service. In the years leading up to war, Training Command began to make use of a large number of North American Harvard trainers, purchased from the USA, and also the predecessor to the Harvard, the Yale. All of the Yale trainers were sent to Canada. Indigenous trainers were obviously heavily used, the ubiquitous Tiger Moth eventually training thousands of pilots from all corners of the Empire, while Magisters and Masters gave the trainee pilots a feel for the high powered combat aircraft to come. These dedicated trainers were soon to be joined by aircraft that were considered no longer useful as front line combat types, such as the Fairey Battle and the Boulton Paul Defiant, but had been produced in such numbers that it became logical to use them for training purposes.

As the different combat types being used by the RAF became ever greater, so too did the training requirements. What started out in 1919 as simply pilot and crew training and aircraft maintenance, this had burgeoned by 1940 into a mass of trades within the RAF that was much, much more. There were Schools for gunnery, wireless, navigation, bomb aiming, electronic warfare, to name just a few. For this reason Training Command was to become two separate units, one being named Flying Training Command, and the other becoming the Technical Training Command.

1940 also saw the creation of the Empire Air Training Scheme, whereby trainee pilots and crew were taught to fly in safer surroundings that were well away from the combat areas. Canada, Rhodesia, New Zealand, Australia and South Africa all contributed to the training of future combat aircrew, and once America had become embroiled in the conflict, it too would train its fair share. The returning aircrew would go to the Operational Training Units and Operational Conversion Units, and from there be assigned to front line Squadrons.

By May 1945, the RAF had over 1 million men, flying and maintaining over 55,000 aircraft of all types. The surprising thing is that of this number, only 20% were frontline combat aircraft, the rest being second line, ancilliary and training aircraft. The end of the Second World War once again saw the RAF facing a massive reduction in men and machines, just like it did in 1919 and 1920, with many Squadrons and Units being disbanded. Likewise, a similar fate befell the Training Squadrons, Flights, Schools, Units, Courses, and so on, many disappearing forever, some to be resurrected at a later date, some surviving and others being re-named. But soon there would be a new skill to master, a new way of flying that would need to be taught, not only to new personnel, but also to the aircrew that chose to stay in the RAF, because the jet age was just around the corner.

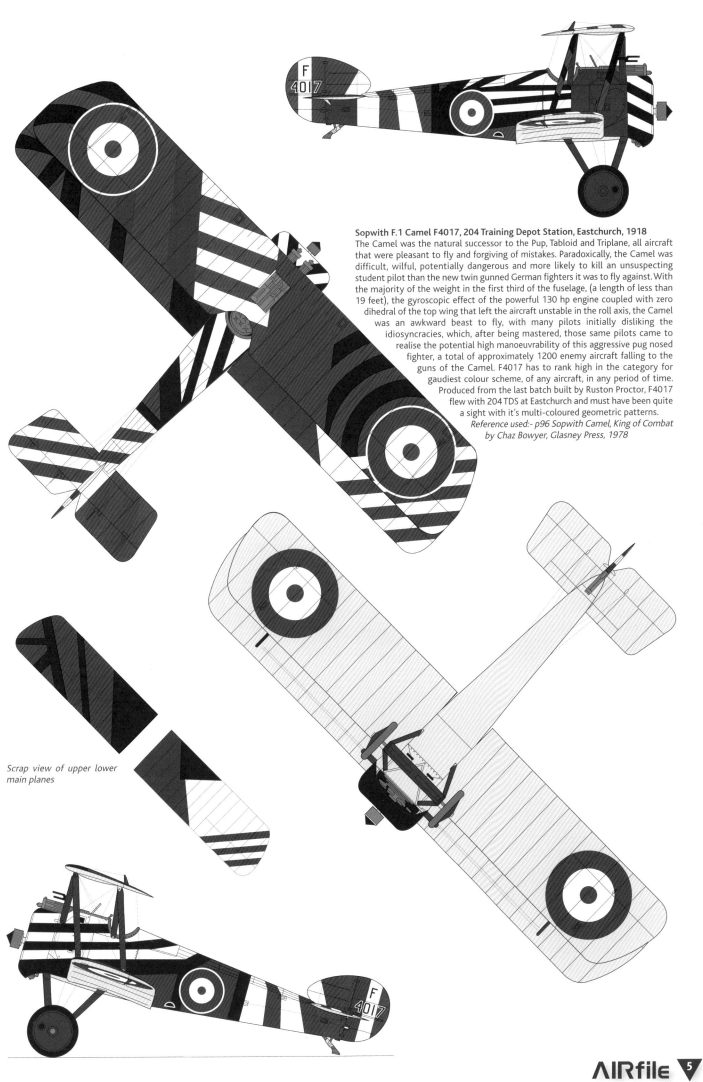

Sopwith F.1 Camel F4017, 204 Training Depot Station, Eastchurch, 1918
The Camel was the natural successor to the Pup, Tabloid and Triplane, all aircraft that were pleasant to fly and forgiving of mistakes. Paradoxically, the Camel was difficult, wilful, potentially dangerous and more likely to kill an unsuspecting student pilot than the new twin gunned German fighters it was to fly against. With the majority of the weight in the first third of the fuselage, (a length of less than 19 feet), the gyroscopic effect of the powerful 130 hp engine coupled with zero dihedral of the top wing that left the aircraft unstable in the roll axis, the Camel was an awkward beast to fly, with many pilots initially disliking the idiosyncracies, which, after being mastered, those same pilots came to realise the potential high manoeuvrability of this aggressive pug nosed fighter, a total of approximately 1200 enemy aircraft falling to the guns of the Camel. F4017 has to rank high in the category for gaudiest colour scheme, of any aircraft, in any period of time. Produced from the last batch built by Ruston Proctor, F4017 flew with 204 TDS at Eastchurch and must have been quite a sight with it's multi-coloured geometric patterns.
Reference used:- p96 Sopwith Camel, King of Combat by Chaz Bowyer, Glasney Press, 1978

Scrap view of upper lower main planes

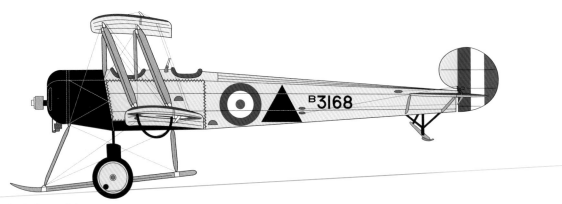

Avro 504J, B3168, School of Special Flying, Gosport 1918
While the 504K was the aircraft that would train the first pilots of the new RAF, there were still examples of the preceding model, the J, continuing to fly. B3168 was one such aircraft, flying at Gosport, the home of the School of Special Flying, created by Major R.R. Smith-Barry, main instigator of the new training regime. B3168 has a variation on the usual colour scheme, with PC10 on the top sides of the flying surfaces only, with the rest in clear doped linen. The triangular marking denotes 'A' Flight and was probably black.
Reference used: p57 The History of Britain's Military Training Aircraft by Ray Sturtivant, Haynes Publishing Group 1987

Scrap view of upper wing surfaces

Bristol M.1C, serial unknown, location unknown, 1918
Not much can be said about this aircraft, as the blue diamond pattern has eliminated the serial. The nose and undercarriage could possibly be black or PC10. Once again, the interpretation of black and white photographs of almost a century ago is difficult, but it is possible that the diamonds were of a light blue colour, or, as here, roundel blue.
Reference used: pp24 and 25 Bristol M.1 by J.M. Bruce, Windsock Datafile 52, Albatros Publications Ltd, 1995

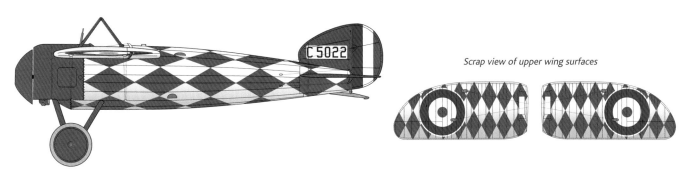

Scrap view of upper wing surfaces

Bristol M.1C, C5022, No.3 Fighting School, Bircham Newton, 1918
Another garish scheme, another diamond pattern, although this time the diamonds are larger and almost certainly red. The high regard the pilots had for these aircraft can be seen in the amazing colour schemes with which they adorned their mounts. No. 3 Fighting School was established in May of 1918, but like most of these early schools was disbanded within a year and re-named, in this case, as No. 7 Training Squadron.
Reference used: p28 Bristol M.1 by J.M. Bruce, Windsock Datafile 52, Albatros Publications Ltd, 1995

Scrap upper plan view of rear fuselage and tailplanes.

Sopwith F.1 Camel B6398 'Sylvestre'. No.10 Training Depot Station, Harling Road, England, October 1918.
After a long and distinguished service career, B6398 was returned to England to take up training duties. Here, the PC10 was quickly changed for a more flambouyant depiction of Cleopatra and her Asp! The colours of this aircraft have been based on known reference of national markings.
Reference used: p101 'Sopwith Camel - King of Combat' by Chaz Bowyer, Glasney Press, 1978

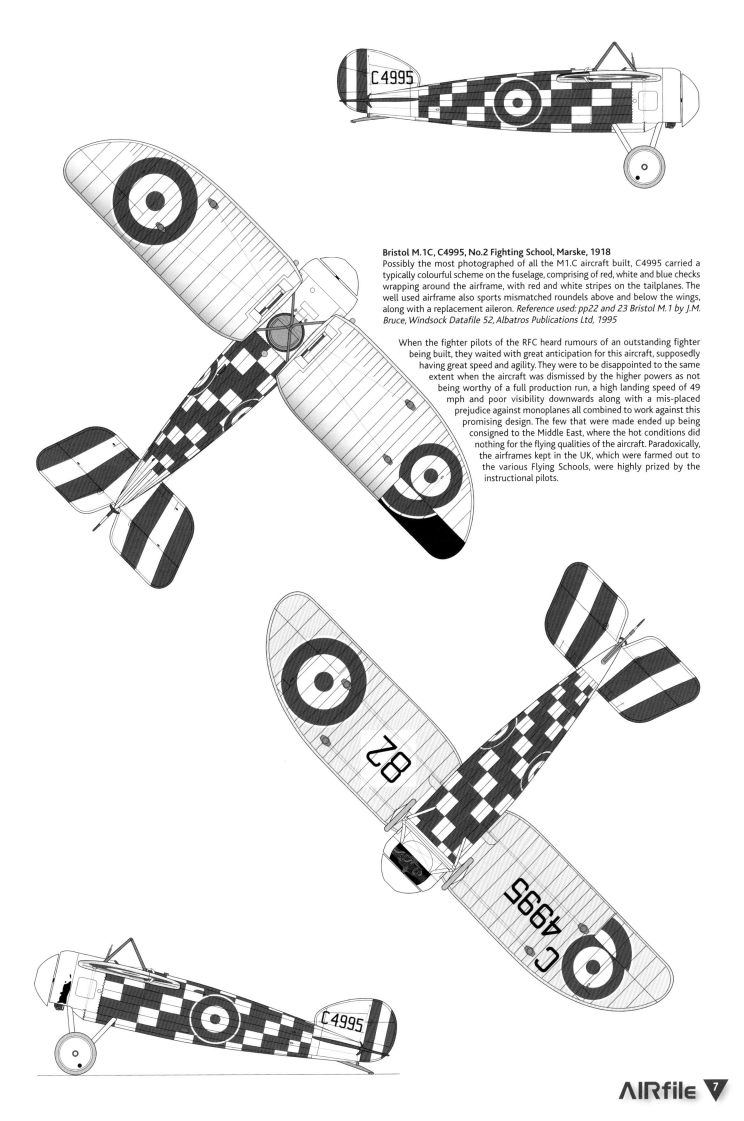

Bristol M.1C, C4995, No.2 Fighting School, Marske, 1918
Possibly the most photographed of all the M1.C aircraft built, C4995 carried a typically colourful scheme on the fuselage, comprising of red, white and blue checks wrapping around the airframe, with red and white stripes on the tailplanes. The well used airframe also sports mismatched roundels above and below the wings, along with a replacement aileron. *Reference used: pp22 and 23 Bristol M.1 by J.M. Bruce, Windsock Datafile 52, Albatros Publications Ltd, 1995*

When the fighter pilots of the RFC heard rumours of an outstanding fighter being built, they waited with great anticipation for this aircraft, supposedly having great speed and agility. They were to be disappointed to the same extent when the aircraft was dismissed by the higher powers as not being worthy of a full production run, a high landing speed of 49 mph and poor visibility downwards along with a mis-placed prejudice against monoplanes all combined to work against this promising design. The few that were made ended up being consigned to the Middle East, where the hot conditions did nothing for the flying qualities of the aircraft. Paradoxically, the airframes kept in the UK, which were farmed out to the various Flying Schools, were highly prized by the instructional pilots.

Scrap view of upper surfaces of upper wing

Sopwith Pup C215, No.54 Training Squadron, Eastbourne, 1918
A possible inhabitant of Eastbourne when 54 Training Squadron was part of 60 Wing, C215 was marked with red, white and blue bands and diamonds on the upper surface of the top wing and fuselage. The addition of the bird motif and name on the fuselage side obviously alluded to the Antipodean origin of the instructor pilot.
Reference used: pp24-25 Sopwith Pup, Windsock Datafile Special by J.M. Bruce, Albatros Publications Ltd, 1992

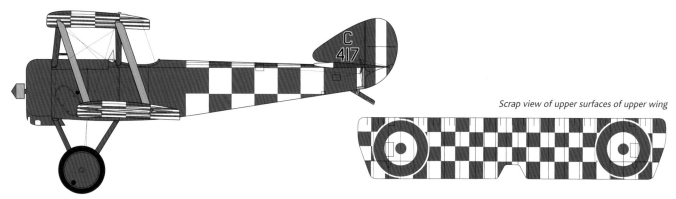

Scrap view of upper surfaces of upper wing

Sopwith Pup C417, No.3 School of Aerial Fighting, Bircham Newton, 1918
Blue and white checks predominate on Pup C417, a variation on an extremely popular post war scheme, even to the extent of eliminating the roundels on the fuselage. All training aircraft that were used by the instructor pilots were well maintained regardless of the age and previous service life.
Reference used: pp26 Sopwith Pup, Windsock Datafile Special by J.M. Bruce, Albatros Publications Ltd, 1992

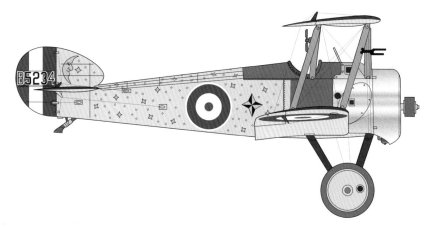

Sopwith F.1 Camel B5234, 'A' Flight, Biggin Hill Wireless Telephony School, 1918
Even as early as 1916 thoughts were turning to the communication of aircraft with the ground. By 1918 several schools had been set up to explore these possibilities, one of them being the Wireless Telephony School at Biggin Hill. B5234, built by Boulton and Paul, was part of 'A' Flight and had the armament removed and a typically colourful fuselage, although whether the moon and stars had anything to do with the role it played at the school is debatable.
Reference used: p97 Sopwith Camel, King of Combat by Chaz Bowyer, Glasney Press, 1978

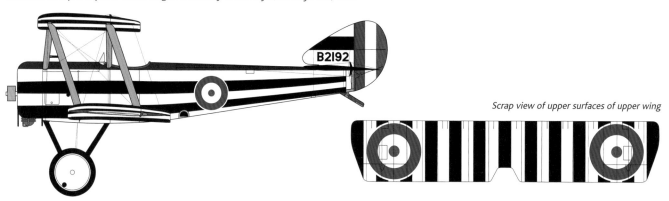

Scrap view of upper surfaces of upper wing

Sopwith Pup B2192, No.1 School of Special Flying, Gosport c.1919
With the Monosoupape engine, the Pup had a short prolonging of frontline service but was soon relegated to the training squadrons. With a striking black and white stripe colour scheme, B2192 was obviously a favoured mount of the instructors at Gosport. The lower quarter of the engine cowl was absent when photographed, either for cooling purposes, engine servicing or, possibly, simply damage.
Reference used: p22 Sopwith Pup, Windsock Datafile Special by J.M. Bruce, Albatros Publications Ltd, 1992

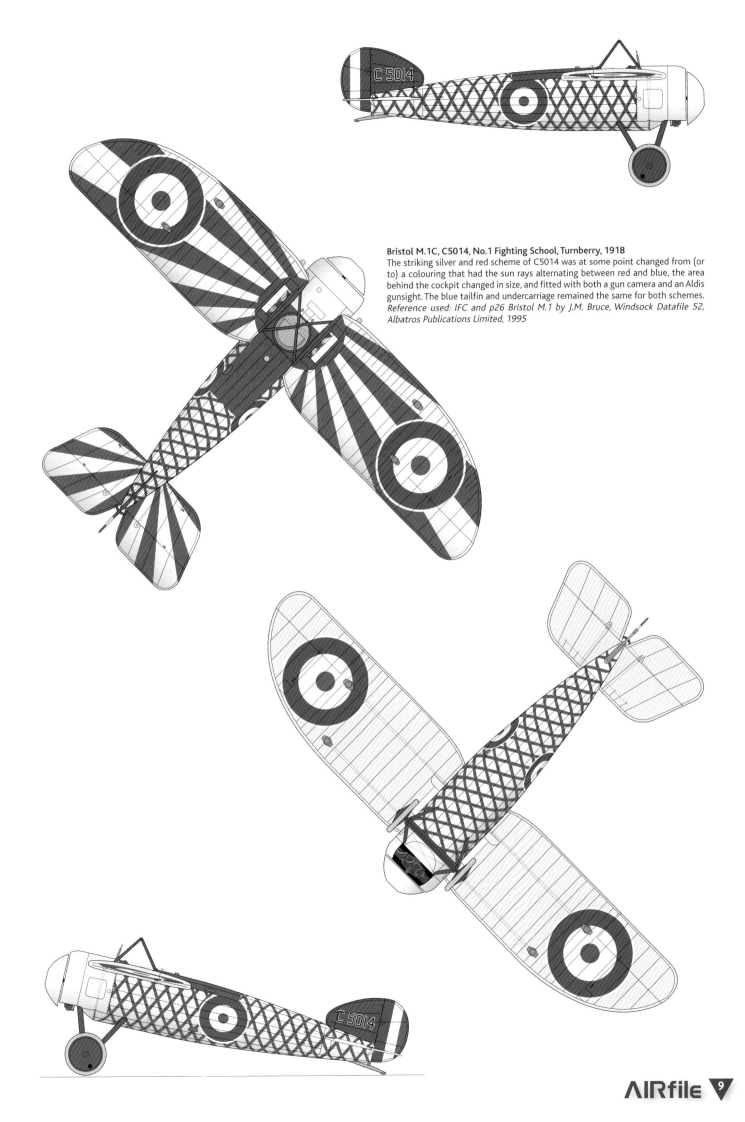

Bristol M.1C, C5014, No.1 Fighting School, Turnberry, 1918
The striking silver and red scheme of C5014 was at some point changed from (or to) a colouring that had the sun rays alternating between red and blue, the area behind the cockpit changed in size, and fitted with both a gun camera and an Aldis gunsight. The blue tailfin and undercarriage remained the same for both schemes.
Reference used: IFC and p26 Bristol M.1 by J.M. Bruce, Windsock Datafile 52, Albatros Publications Limited, 1995

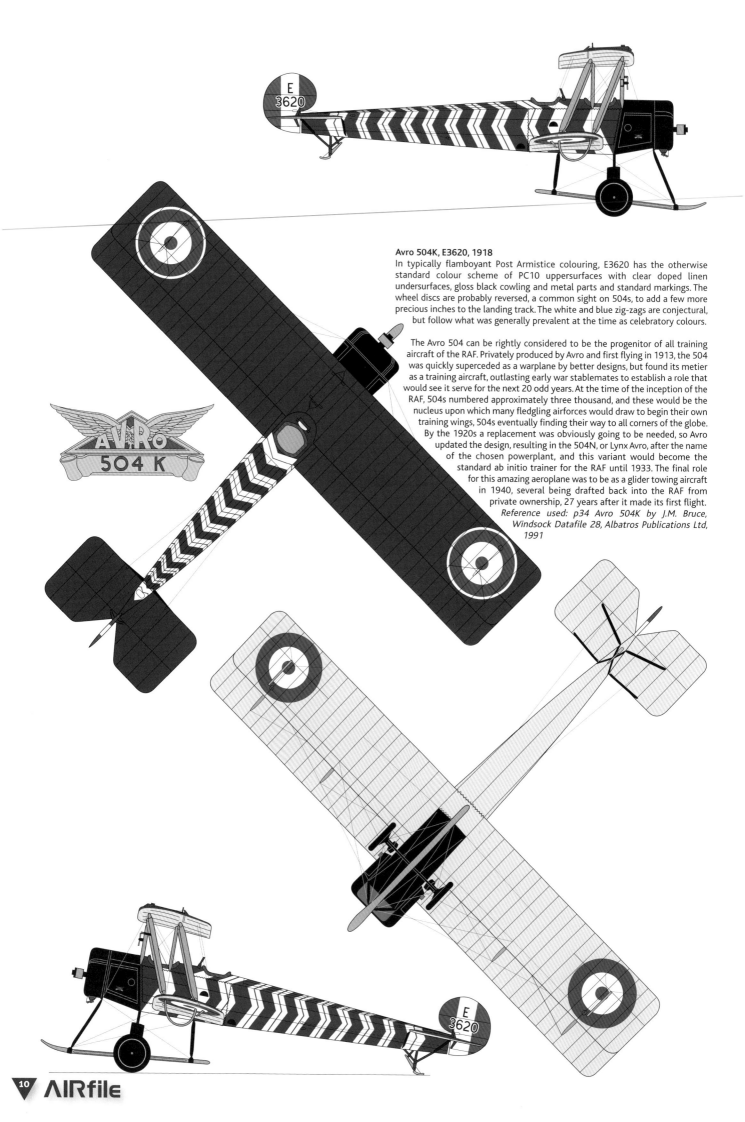

Avro 504K, E3620, 1918

In typically flamboyant Post Armistice colouring, E3620 has the otherwise standard colour scheme of PC10 uppersurfaces with clear doped linen undersurfaces, gloss black cowling and metal parts and standard markings. The wheel discs are probably reversed, a common sight on 504s, to add a few more precious inches to the landing track. The white and blue zig-zags are conjectural, but follow what was generally prevalent at the time as celebratory colours.

The Avro 504 can be rightly considered to be the progenitor of all training aircraft of the RAF. Privately produced by Avro and first flying in 1913, the 504 was quickly superceded as a warplane by better designs, but found its metier as a training aircraft, outlasting early war stablemates to establish a role that would see it serve for the next 20 odd years. At the time of the inception of the RAF, 504s numbered approximately three thousand, and these would be the nucleus upon which many fledgling airforces would draw to begin their own training wings, 504s eventually finding their way to all corners of the globe. By the 1920s a replacement was obviously going to be needed, so Avro updated the design, resulting in the 504N, or Lynx Avro, after the name of the chosen powerplant, and this variant would become the standard ab initio trainer for the RAF until 1933. The final role for this amazing aeroplane was to be as a glider towing aircraft in 1940, several being drafted back into the RAF from private ownership, 27 years after it made its first flight.
Reference used: p34 Avro 504K by J.M. Bruce, Windsock Datafile 28, Albatros Publications Ltd, 1991

Sopwith Pup C242, No.7 Training Squadron, Netheravon, 1918
While the De Havilland DH 2 did much to redress the balance of air power by curtailing the short but deadly success of the Fokker Eindecker, it was not until the arrival of the Sopwith Pup that the RFC had an aircraft that could be truly regarded as a fighter in the classic sense. Pups began to arrive in France late in 1916 and pilots quickly found it to be manoeuvrable without being difficult to fly, a trait that made it extremely popular with the front line pilots, and later, with the instructional pilots of the Fighting Schools, where it was highly prized. C242 had an elaborate Harlequin colour scheme overall, on all surfaces, which must have taken quite a while to apply by some unfortunate mechanic/rigger.
Reference used: p25 Sopwith Pup, Windsock Datafile Special by J.M. Bruce, Albatros Publications Ltd, 1992

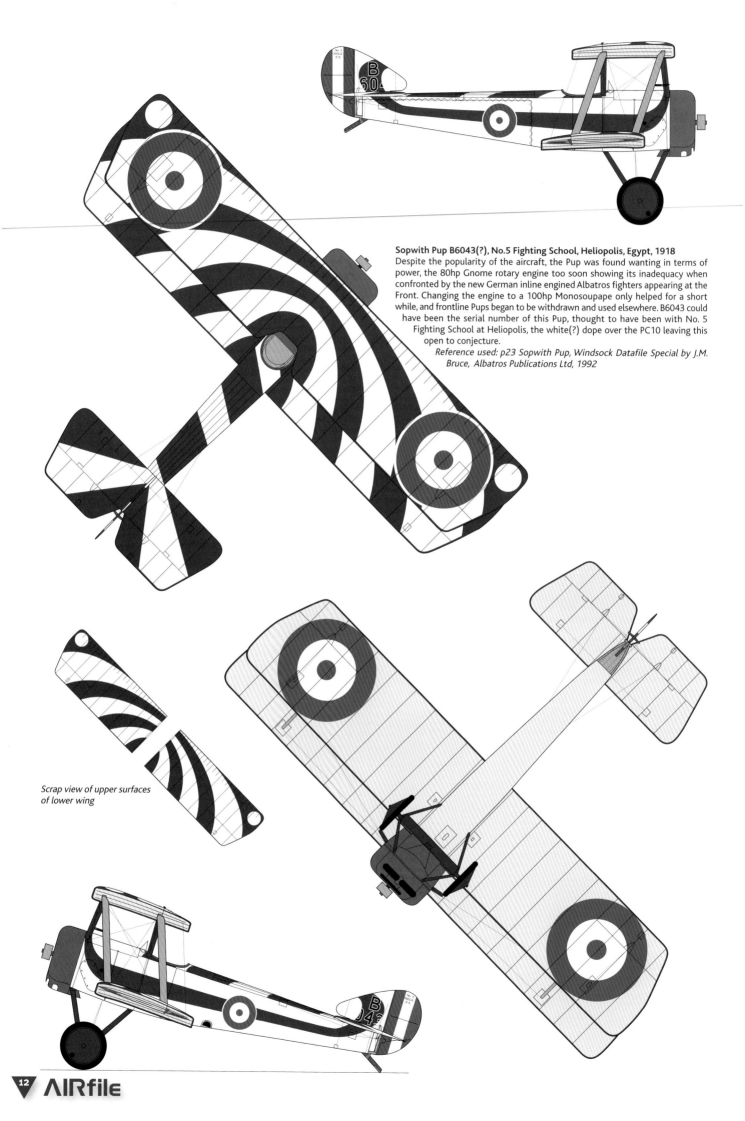

Sopwith Pup B6043(?), No.5 Fighting School, Heliopolis, Egypt, 1918
Despite the popularity of the aircraft, the Pup was found wanting in terms of
power, the 80hp Gnome rotary engine too soon showing its inadequacy when
confronted by the new German inline engined Albatros fighters appearing at the
Front. Changing the engine to a 100hp Monosoupape only helped for a short
while, and frontline Pups began to be withdrawn and used elsewhere. B6043 could
have been the serial number of this Pup, thought to have been with No. 5
Fighting School at Heliopolis, the white(?) dope over the PC10 leaving this
open to conjecture.
*Reference used: p23 Sopwith Pup, Windsock Datafile Special by J.M.
Bruce, Albatros Publications Ltd, 1992*

*Scrap view of upper surfaces
of lower wing*

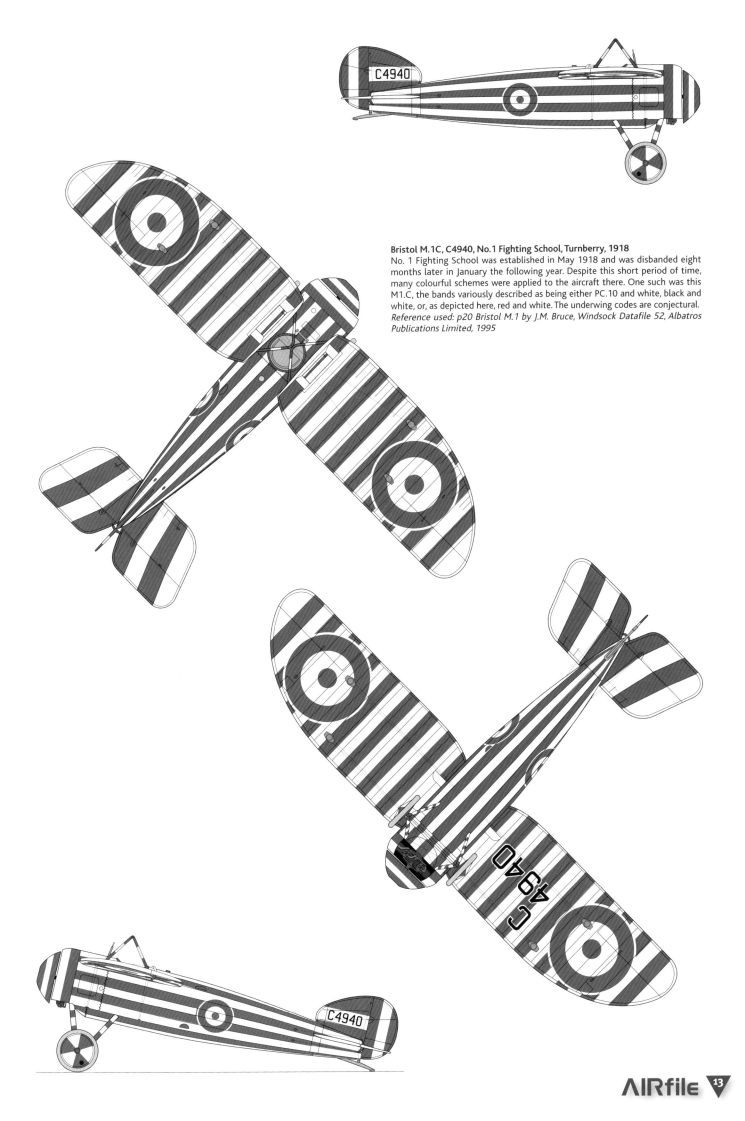

Bristol M.1C, C4940, No.1 Fighting School, Turnberry, 1918
No. 1 Fighting School was established in May 1918 and was disbanded eight months later in January the following year. Despite this short period of time, many colourful schemes were applied to the aircraft there. One such was this M1.C, the bands variously described as being either PC.10 and white, black and white, or, as depicted here, red and white. The underwing codes are conjectural.
Reference used: p20 Bristol M.1 by J.M. Bruce, Windsock Datafile 52, Albatros Publications Limited, 1995

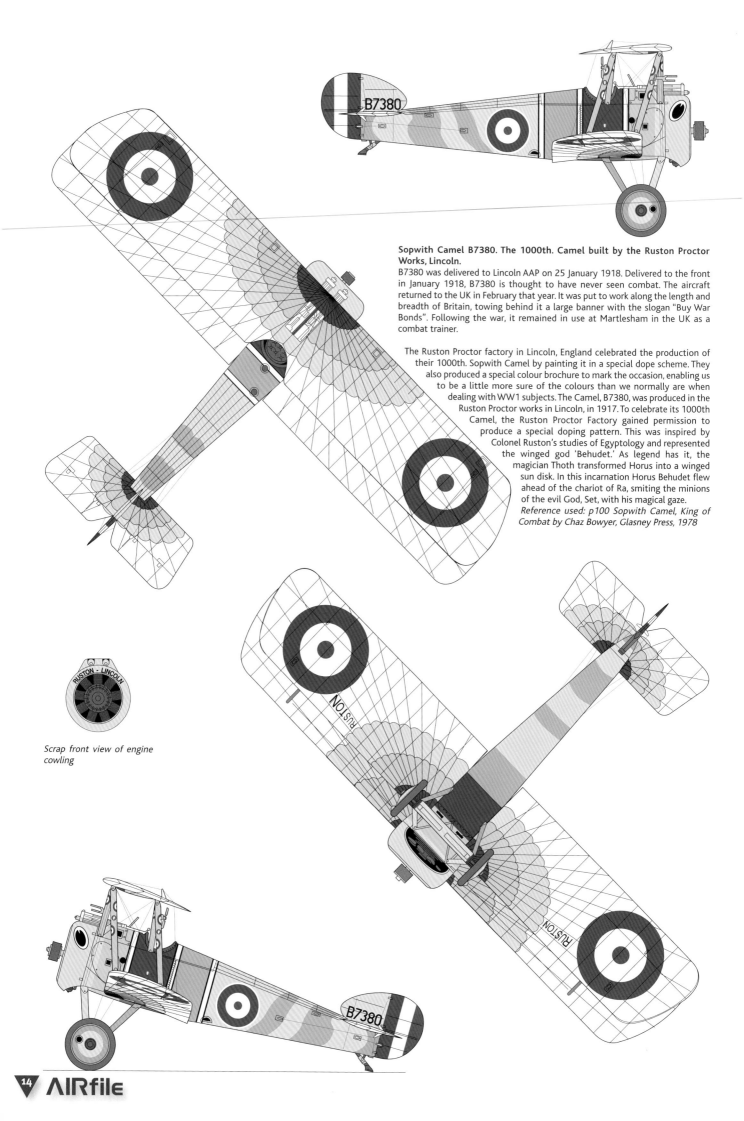

Sopwith Camel B7380. The 1000th. Camel built by the Ruston Proctor Works, Lincoln.

B7380 was delivered to Lincoln AAP on 25 January 1918. Delivered to the front in January 1918, B7380 is thought to have never seen combat. The aircraft returned to the UK in February that year. It was put to work along the length and breadth of Britain, towing behind it a large banner with the slogan "Buy War Bonds". Following the war, it remained in use at Martlesham in the UK as a combat trainer.

The Ruston Proctor factory in Lincoln, England celebrated the production of their 1000th. Sopwith Camel by painting it in a special dope scheme. They also produced a special colour brochure to mark the occasion, enabling us to be a little more sure of the colours than we normally are when dealing with WW1 subjects. The Camel, B7380, was produced in the Ruston Proctor works in Lincoln, in 1917. To celebrate its 1000th Camel, the Ruston Proctor Factory gained permission to produce a special doping pattern. This was inspired by Colonel Ruston's studies of Egyptology and represented the winged god 'Behudet.' As legend has it, the magician Thoth transformed Horus into a winged sun disk. In this incarnation Horus Behudet flew ahead of the chariot of Ra, smiting the minions of the evil God, Set, with his magical gaze.
Reference used: p100 Sopwith Camel, King of Combat by Chaz Bowyer, Glasney Press, 1978

Scrap front view of engine cowling

Bristol Fighter F2B, C4879, No. 33 Training Depot Station, Witney, 1918
The checker board design of C4879 went through various stages before resulting in the final scheme depicted here, different guises showing it with plain top surfaces to the lower wings and plain undersides to the upper wing. When photographed at Witney both of these surfaces were covered in black checks, and the tailfin carried the code on the left hand side, reversed out of the black and white, although it cannot be confirmed if the code was also on the right hand side at this point in time.
Reference used: p26 The History of Britain's Military Training Aircraft by Ray Sturtivant, Haynes Publishing Group 1987

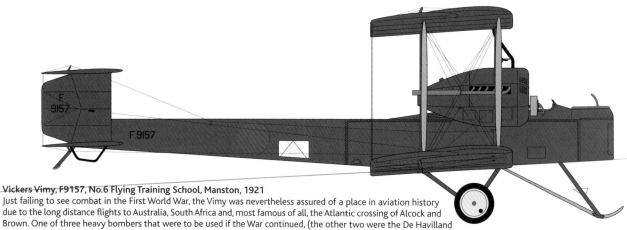

Vickers Vimy, F9157, No.6 Flying Training School, Manston, 1921

Just failing to see combat in the First World War, the Vimy was nevertheless assured of a place in aviation history due to the long distance flights to Australia, South Africa and, most famous of all, the Atlantic crossing of Alcock and Brown. One of three heavy bombers that were to be used if the War continued, (the other two were the De Havilland DH 10 Amiens and the Handley Page V/1500), the Vimy was the only one to enjoy a respectable period of time in service with the RAF post Armistice, being the standard heavy bomber until 1925. F.9157 was captured on film at Manston in 1921 and had the newer camouflage colour of NIVO overall, with the roundels in red and blue.

Reference used: p12 Vickers Vimy by J.M. Bruce, Albatros Publications Ltd, 1994

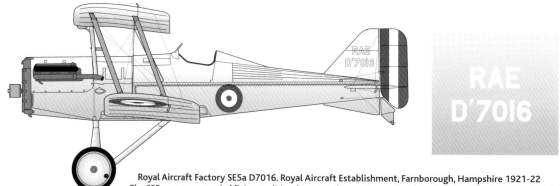

Royal Aircraft Factory SE5a D7016. Royal Aircraft Establishment, Farnborough, Hampshire 1921-22

The SE5a was possessed of flying qualities that were the exact opposite of the Sopwith Camel, an aircraft that it will be forever compared with. It was easy to fly, strongly built and made for an extremely stable gun platform, so stable in fact that it had the ability to hang by the propellor, a trick that the Camel could never hope to emulate. D'7016 was probably built just after the end of the Great War, around 1919, and unlike many other SE5a's, managed to survive into the 1930s as a racer. The period illustrated here was the early 1920s, when it was flying with the RAE, devoid of armament and doped silver overall, with the tailcode applied in white. The side view has a black outline to the code for purposes of clarity; the enlarged view of the tailfin shows how the code number was actually rendered on the airframe.

Reference used: p19 'RAF SE5a' by J.M Bruce, Windsock Datafile Special, Albatros Publications Ltd, 1993

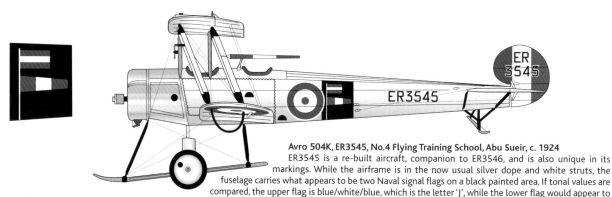

Avro 504K, ER3545, No.4 Flying Training School, Abu Sueir, c. 1924

ER3545 is a re-built aircraft, companion to ER3546, and is also unique in its markings. While the airframe is in the now usual silver dope and white struts, the fuselage carries what appears to be two Naval signal flags on a black painted area. If tonal values are compared, the upper flag is blue/white/blue, which is the letter 'J', while the lower flag would appear to be red/white/ blue, signifying the number '3'. Unfortunately, the significance or meaning of this marking has long since been forgotten. Also of note is the streamer attached to the port strut.

Reference used: p58 The History of Britain's Military Training Aircraft by Ray Sturtivant, Haynes Publishing Group 1987

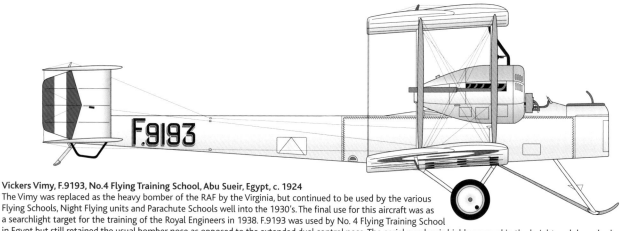

Vickers Vimy, F.9193, No.4 Flying Training School, Abu Sueir, Egypt, c. 1924

The Vimy was replaced as the heavy bomber of the RAF by the Virginia, but continued to be used by the various Flying Schools, Night Flying units and Parachute Schools well into the 1930's. The final use for this aircraft was as a searchlight target for the training of the Royal Engineers in 1938. F.9193 was used by No. 4 Flying Training School in Egypt but still retained the usual bomber nose as opposed to the extended dual control nose. The serial number is highly unusual in the height and drop shadow style used.

Reference used: p15 Vickers Vimy by J.M. Bruce, Albatros Publications Ltd, 1994

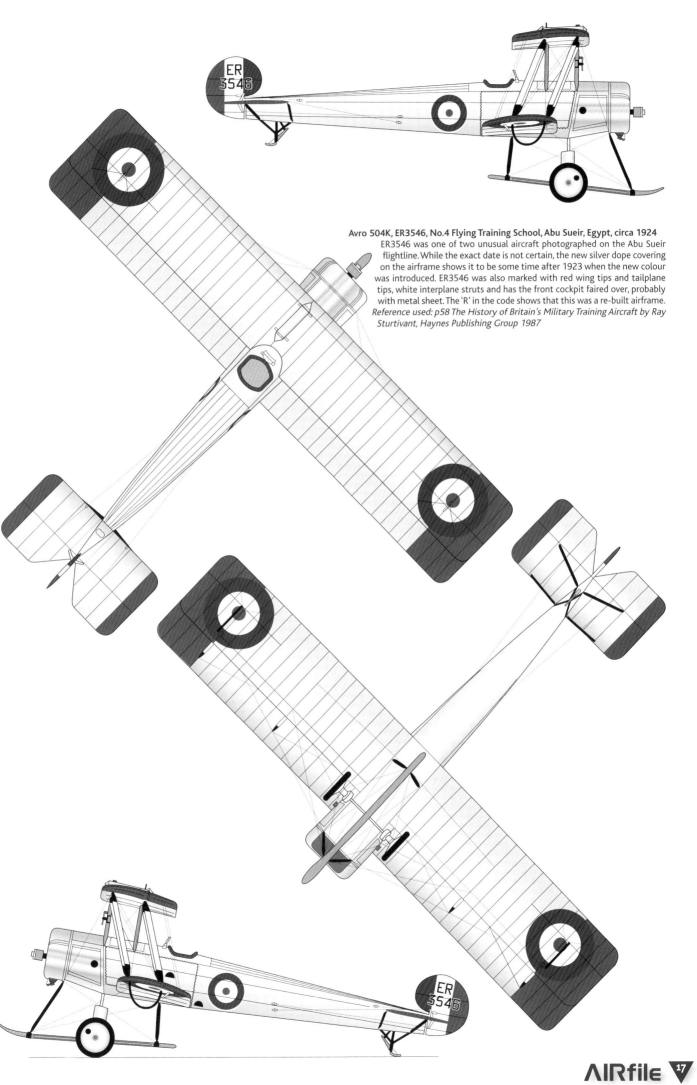

Avro 504K, ER3546, No.4 Flying Training School, Abu Sueir, Egypt, circa 1924
ER3546 was one of two unusual aircraft photographed on the Abu Sueir
flightline. While the exact date is not certain, the new silver dope covering
on the airframe shows it to be some time after 1923 when the new colour
was introduced. ER3546 was also marked with red wing tips and tailplane
tips, white interplane struts and has the front cockpit faired over, probably
with metal sheet. The 'R' in the code shows that this was a re-built airframe.
*Reference used: p58 The History of Britain's Military Training Aircraft by Ray
Sturtivant, Haynes Publishing Group 1987*

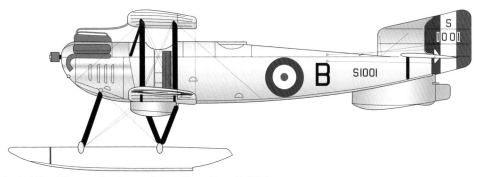

Fairey IIID S1001 'B'. School of Naval Co-operation, Lee-on-Solent, Hampshire mid 1920's
The School of Naval Co-operation was initially formed in 1919 as the RAF & Naval Co-operation School at Lee-on-Solent. In May 1923 it was re-formed as the School of Naval Co-operation to provide training for floatplane and amphibious pilots of the Fleet Air Arm. During the 1920's, the Fairey IIID and IIIF were the primary aircraft types used by the School, particularly for their good flying qualities and reliability. While most of the twin floatplane IIID's went to the Royal Navy, the wheeled landplane version was equally popular with the RAF. It was four RAF Fairey IIIDs that made the first historic flight from Cairo, Egypt, to Cape Town, South Africa in March 1926 and returning to England via Europe in June of that year having covered a total of 13,901 miles without mechanical failure of any kind!
Reference used: www.daveg4otu.tripod.com/airfields/los.html

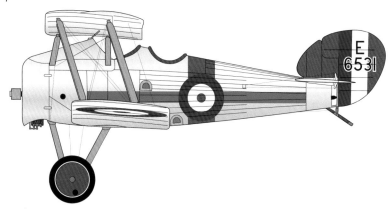

Sopwith 7F.1 Snipe, E6531. No.3 Squadron, Upavon, 1925
Built by Boulton and Paul, E6531 was one of approximately 40 Snipe airframes that were converted by the Hawker company into dual control trainers, some going to the Flying Schools, and some, like this one, on strength with the front line squadrons. Endurance time must have been very limited, as the second seat behind the original cockpit occupied the space normally taken by the fuel tank, although the removal of the guns would have helped.
Reference used: p23 Sopwith Snipe by J.M. Bruce, Windsock Datafile 46, Albatros Publications Limited, 1994

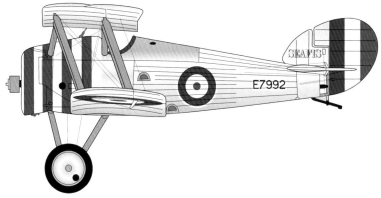

Sopwith 7F.1 Snipe, E7992, South Eastern Area Flying Instructors School, Shoreham, c.1925
With the acronym on the tailfin stating clearly the School to which it belonged, E7992 was photographed in the short period of time that the South Eastern Area Flying Instructors School existed, a mere eight months from July 1918 to the end of March 1919. The unusual markings include a standard Sopwith style white background rectangle to the black code number, despite the silver finish, and coloured bands to the nose and cowl, possibly denoting a senior officers aircraft.
Reference used: p34 Sopwith Snipe by J.M. Bruce, Windsock Datafile 46, Albatros Publications Limited, 1994

Sopwith 7F.1 Snipe, E6335, Central Flying School, Upavon, c.1926
From the same manufacturer and batch as the earlier two seat aircraft, E6335 was also known to have been at Wittering. The unusual feature of this aircraft is the fuselage code number being the same size as the rudder code. By 1926 the use of Snipes was coming to a close, the 1100 aircraft built having soldiered on long past the time they should have been retired. As a replacement for the Camel, the Snipe was never quite as good, but was around in sufficient numbers to see the new RAF through the post war period when there was a great reduction in fighter aircraft.
Reference used: p147 Royal Air Force Fighters 1920-1929 by J.D.R. Rawlings, Wings of Fame Volume 5, Aerospace Publications, 1996

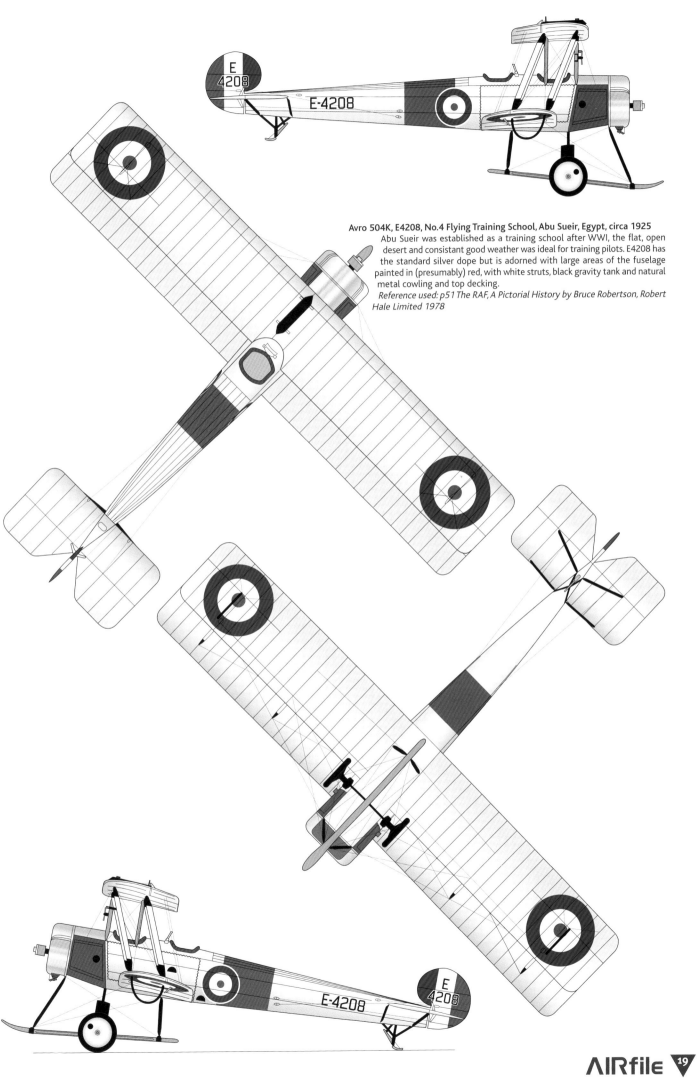

Avro 504K, E4208, No.4 Flying Training School, Abu Sueir, Egypt, circa 1925
Abu Sueir was established as a training school after WWI, the flat, open desert and consistant good weather was ideal for training pilots. E4208 has the standard silver dope but is adorned with large areas of the fuselage painted in (presumably) red, with white struts, black gravity tank and natural metal cowling and top decking.
Reference used: p51 The RAF, A Pictorial History by Bruce Robertson, Robert Hale Limited 1978

E-4208

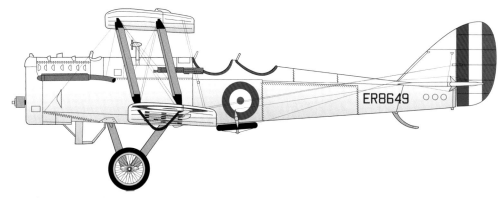

Airco DH9A ER8649. No.4 Flying Training School, Abu Sueir, Egypt 1926.
The 'Ninak' was a development of the unpopular and under-powered DH9, an aircraft from which great things had been expected towards the end of the Great War, but failed, primarily because of the Puma engine. This was replaced by either the Rolls Royce Eagle or the American Liberty engine, allowing the otherwise acceptable airframe to realise the full potential of a design that would go on to give the RAF 13 years service. One of many aircraft used by No.4 FTS in Egypt, ER8649 was initially built by the parent company, and was possibly converted to a two-seat configuration by Westland, the letter 'R' in the serial showing this to be a re-conditioned airframe. Middle East Ninaks were well known for their (necessary) add-ons to the fuselage, so with just an under-nose radiator and spare wheel, ER8649 looks comparatively clean.
Reference used: p64 'De Havilland DH9/9A' by Ken Wixey, Fly Past Magazine, May 1984

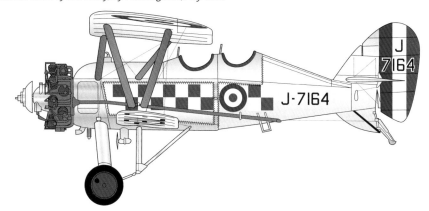

Armstrong Whitworth Siskin IIIDC J-7164. 56 Squadron, RAF North Weald, late 1920s
Each Siskin squadron was allocated at least one dual control, two-seat trainer. Most of these were converted Siskin IIIs. The squadron marking of red and white chequers along the fuselage would have been repeated across the top wing.
Reference used: http://en.wikipedia.org/wiki.No_56_Squadron_RAF

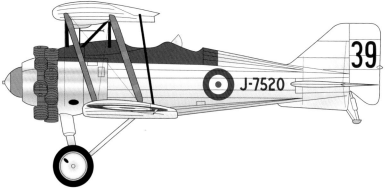

Gloster Grebe III DC J-7520, Central Flying School, Wittering, 1928
J-7520 was the second Grebe built as a two seat Dual Control aircraft, and served in that capacity with Nos. 25 and 29 Squadrons. It was as a competitor that J-7520 achieved a modicum of fame, as it was entered as aircraft number 23 in the 1928 Kings Cup Air Race but did not win. A year later the aircraft was entered again, with the race number 39 and was victorious.
Reference used: p102 'Gloster Aircraft since 1917' by Derek N. James, Putnam & Company Ltd, 1971

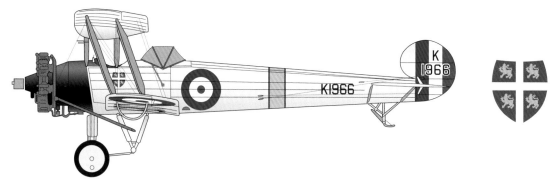

Avro 504N K1966 Cambridge University Air Squadron, Netheravon Annual Camp, 1933
Cambridge University was the first English university to form an air squadron in October 1925. The trainee pilots were all undergraduates of the University, following a basic flying syllabus on a part-time basis between their normal studies. K1966 carries the distinctive 'Cambridge Blue' light blue band outlined in darker blue around the fuselage and also the University coat of arms which is incorporated into its squadron badge below the front cockpit. Note the closed blind flying hood over the rear cockpit, indicating the trainee was undertaking a flying by instruments only exercise.
Reference used: p60 The History of Britain's Military Training Aircraft by Ray Sturtivant, Haynes Publishing Group 1987

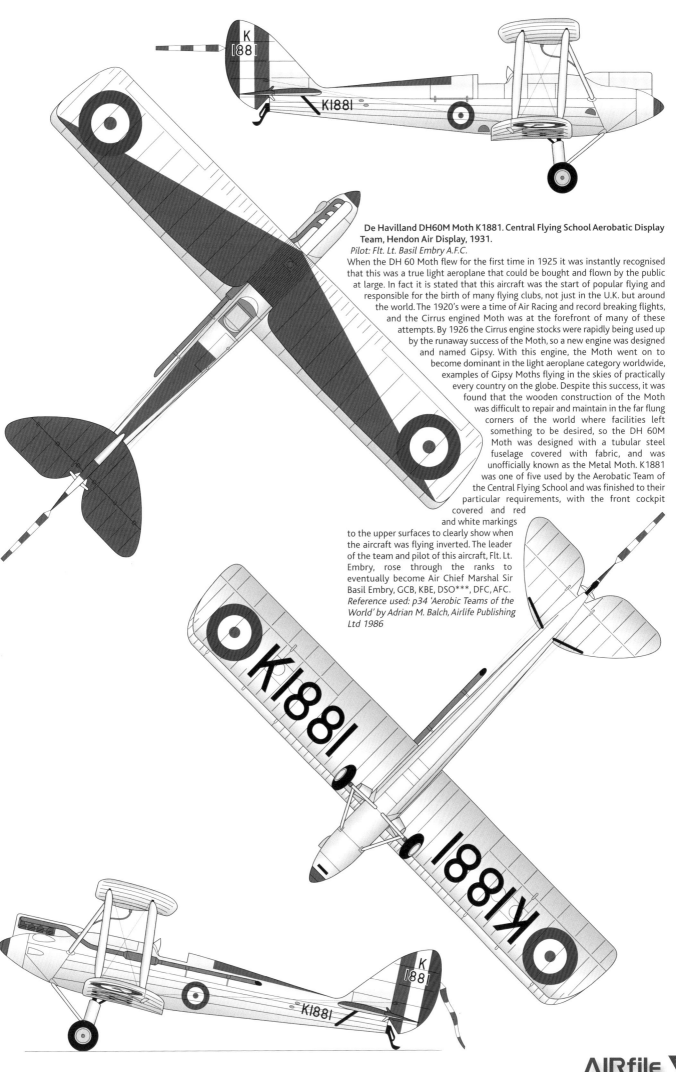

De Havilland DH60M Moth K1881. Central Flying School Aerobatic Display Team, Hendon Air Display, 1931.

Pilot: Flt. Lt. Basil Embry A.F.C.

When the DH 60 Moth flew for the first time in 1925 it was instantly recognised that this was a true light aeroplane that could be bought and flown by the public at large. In fact it is stated that this aircraft was the start of popular flying and responsible for the birth of many flying clubs, not just in the U.K. but around the world. The 1920's were a time of Air Racing and record breaking flights, and the Cirrus engined Moth was at the forefront of many of these attempts. By 1926 the Cirrus engine stocks were rapidly being used up by the runaway success of the Moth, so a new engine was designed and named Gipsy. With this engine, the Moth went on to become dominant in the light aeroplane category worldwide, examples of Gipsy Moths flying in the skies of practically every country on the globe. Despite this success, it was found that the wooden construction of the Moth was difficult to repair and maintain in the far flung corners of the world where facilities left something to be desired, so the DH 60M Moth was designed with a tubular steel fuselage covered with fabric, and was unofficially known as the Metal Moth. K1881 was one of five used by the Aerobatic Team of the Central Flying School and was finished to their particular requirements, with the front cockpit covered and red and white markings to the upper surfaces to clearly show when the aircraft was flying inverted. The leader of the team and pilot of this aircraft, Flt. Lt. Embry, rose through the ranks to eventually become Air Chief Marshal Sir Basil Embry, GCB, KBE, DSO***, DFC, AFC.

Reference used: p34 'Aerobic Teams of the World' by Adrian M. Balch, Airlife Publishing Ltd 1986

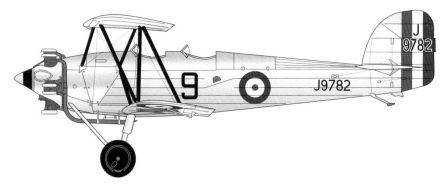

Hawker Tomtit J9782 '9'. No.3 Flying Training School, Grantham, early 1930's
The Tomtit was an attempt by the Hawker Company to enter the field of producing trainers for the RAF. For a trainer it was advanced for the period, so much so that despite innovative features such as metal construction, blind flying panel, adjustable blind flying hood and automatic slots in the upper wing leading edge, these features worked against the design as regards cost, resulting in only 25 examples being used by the RAF. The only relief from an otherwise standard silver finish is the black number 9 on the side of J9782, most likely an identification number used by No.3 FTS at Grantham.
Reference used: p318 'Aircraft of the Royal Air Force since 1918' by Owen Thetford, Putnam 1976

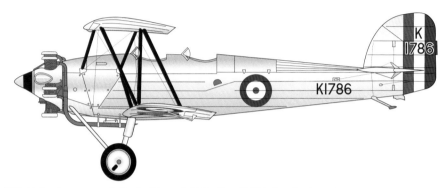

Hawker Tomtit K1786/G-AFTA. Unit unknown, now in the Shuttleworth Collection, Old Warden, Biggleswade
K1786 was the last Hawker Tomtit to be built in 1931 out of 25 produced for the RAF.from 1929 to 1932 Tomtits were in service with No.3 FTS, Grantham, the Central Flying School at Wittering and a few were used for communication duties by No.24 Squadron at Northolt. While not much of its early history can be confirmed, it is known that K1786 was used as a 'hack' by Alec Henshaw during the Second World War. It was owned by Neville Duke who displayed it regularly until being purchased by Hawker Aircraft in 1951.It was presented to the Shuttleworth Collection in 1956 who have restored it to its original colours and flying condition.
Reference used: http://en.wikipedia.org/wiki/Hawker_Tomtit

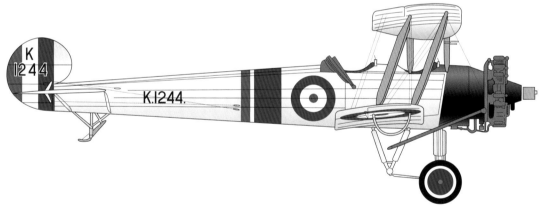

Avro 504N, K1244, Central Flying School, Wittering, 1931
The 504N can lay claim to be the very first instrument trainer, when in 1931 blind flying hoods and instruments were fitted to aircraft at the Central Flying School at Wittering. K1244 had fuselage bands of red and blue, possibly to show that this was an instrument trainer.
Reference used: p7 Aeroplane Monthly, Volume 3, Number 1, Flight International, 1975

De Havilland DH82 Tiger Moth K-2579 '9'. No.3 Flying Training School, Grantham, 1932
One of the first 35 aircraft built, K-2579 was sent to No.3 Flying Training School at Grantham, the first recipients of an aeroplane that would soon populate every flying school in the land. Being an early airframe, K-2579 would have had the Gipsy III engine and the aft fuselage would have been fabric covered. The overall silver colour scheme was prevalent for the 1930's and the red white blue rudder stripes would last only another two years, being dispensed with by 1934.
Reference used: p303 'De Havilland Aircraft since 1909' by A. J. Jackson, Putnam & Company Limited, 1962

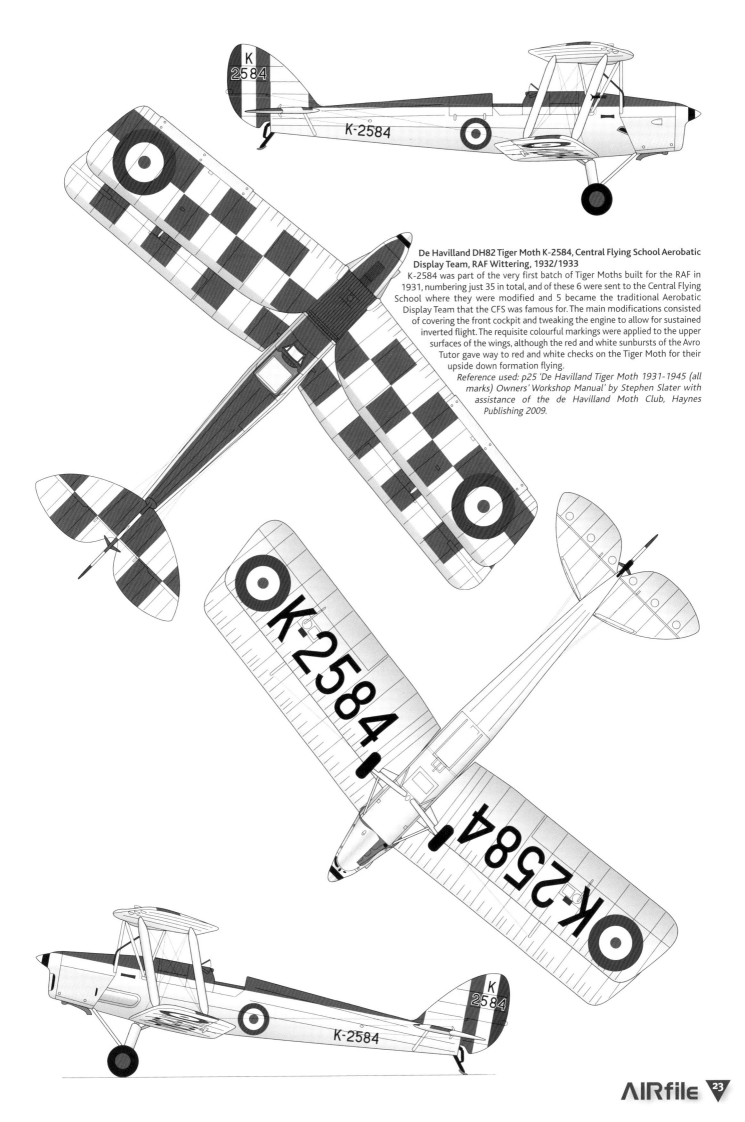

De Havilland DH82 Tiger Moth K-2584, Central Flying School Aerobatic Display Team, RAF Wittering, 1932/1933

K-2584 was part of the very first batch of Tiger Moths built for the RAF in 1931, numbering just 35 in total, and of these 6 were sent to the Central Flying School where they were modified and 5 became the traditional Aerobatic Display Team that the CFS was famous for. The main modifications consisted of covering the front cockpit and tweaking the engine to allow for sustained inverted flight. The requisite colourful markings were applied to the upper surfaces of the wings, although the red and white sunbursts of the Avro Tutor gave way to red and white checks on the Tiger Moth for their upside down formation flying.

Reference used: p25 'De Havilland Tiger Moth 1931-1945 (all marks) Owners' Workshop Manual' by Stephen Slater with assistance of the de Havilland Moth Club, Haynes Publishing 2009.

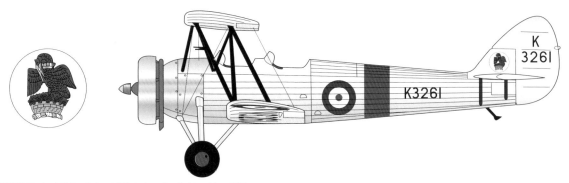

Avro Tutor K3261 Central Flying School, Wittering, Cambridgeshire 1933
The Central Flying School were the first to receive the Avro Tutor in 1932. The aircraft was chosen, after extensive trials, to replace the ageing Avro 504K, J and N biplanes which had provided service since the end of the First World War. By 1934 the Avro Tutor had become the standard trainer at all the RAF Flying Training Schools and with the University Air Squadrons until 1939.
Reference used: p52 Aircraft of the Royal Air Force since 1918' by Owen Thetford, Guild Publishing, London, 1988

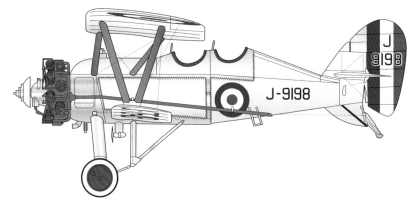

Armstrong Whitworth Siskin IIIA (DC), J-9198, No. 5 Flying Training School, Sealand, 1933
J-9198 was one of 47 Dual Control Siskin aircraft built specifically as two seat trainers, as opposed to the 30 plus conversions from single seat aircraft. This particular aircraft seemed to give good value for money, as it served with Nos. 111, 25 and 54 Squadrons, before moving to the Royal Air Force Training Base at Leuchars, where it was part of 'B' Flight, training spotters, before ending up at Sealand in 1933.
Reference used: p29 The History of Britain's Military Training Aircraft by Ray Sturtivant, Haynes Publishing Group 1987

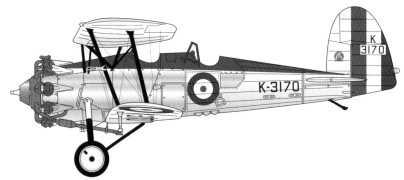

Bristol Bulldog TM K3170. Central Flying School, Wittering, 1934.
K-3170 was the first aircraft of a production batch of 69 aircraft. The Bulldog TM was the training version of the Bristol Bulldog single-seat fighter. It incorporated a second cockpit with dual controls, but with no armament. The rear fuselage could be replaced by a standard fighter rear fuselage and there was provision for the installation of machine guns so that the TM could be rapidly converted into a fighter if required. The Bulldog TM remained in RAF service with training schools until 1939.
Reference used: p135 Aircraft of the Royal Air Force since 1918' by Owen Thetford, Guild Publishing, London, 1988

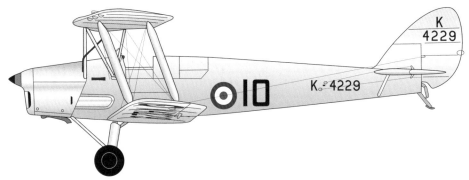

De Havilland DH82B Queen Bee K4229 '10', No. 1 Gunnery Co-operation Flight, Farnborough, Hampshire 1934
The Queen Bee was the world's first practical aerial target. The company designation may lead some to think that it was a variant of the DH 82A Tiger Moth, when in fact it was more of a hybrid aircraft, with the wings and undercarriage (when fitted) of a Tiger Moth, but with the fuselage and engine of a Moth Major. The fuselage was of plywood covering a wooden internal frame, to keep interference with the electrical signals to a minimum, and to allow some bouyancy when coming down in the sea, for all Queen Bee aircraft were shot at over open water. The receiving equipment was stored in the aft cockpit and powered by a windmill generator fixed to the port cabane strut. The standard wheeled undercarriage (shown here) was usually only used when the aircraft was being delivered, or on test, twin floats normally used when at sea.
Reference used: p157 'RAF Flying Training and Support Units since 1912' by Ray Sturtivant with John Hamlin, Air-Britain (Historians) Ltd 2007

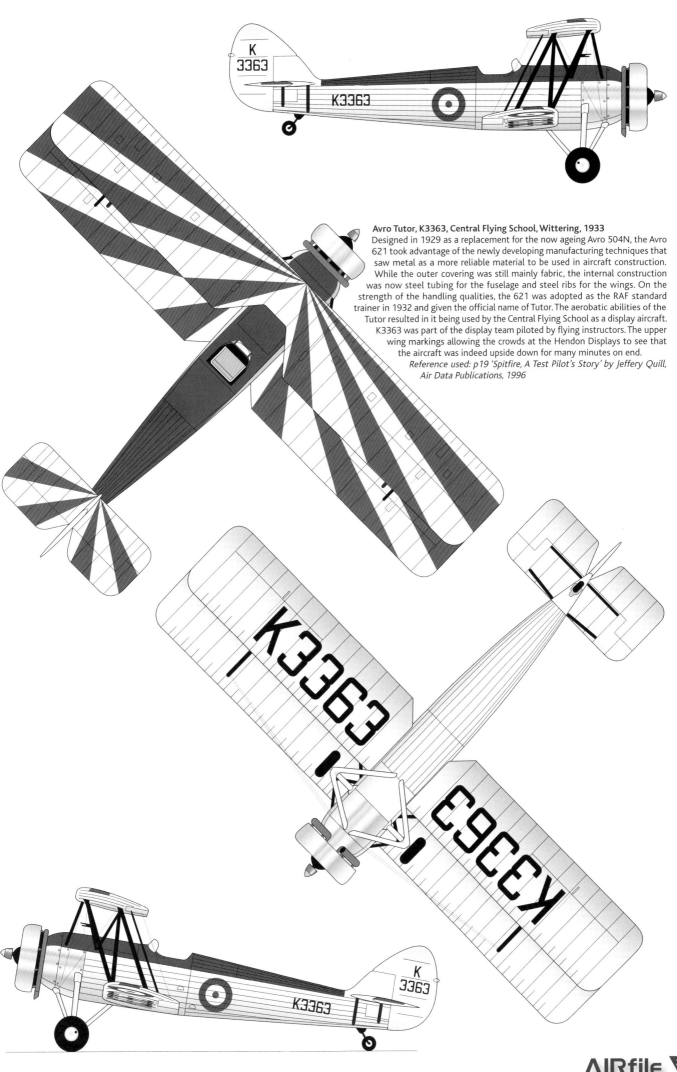

Avro Tutor, K3363, Central Flying School, Wittering, 1933
Designed in 1929 as a replacement for the now ageing Avro 504N, the Avro 621 took advantage of the newly developing manufacturing techniques that saw metal as a more reliable material to be used in aircraft construction. While the outer covering was still mainly fabric, the internal construction was now steel tubing for the fuselage and steel ribs for the wings. On the strength of the handling qualities, the 621 was adopted as the RAF standard trainer in 1932 and given the official name of Tutor. The aerobatic abilities of the Tutor resulted in it being used by the Central Flying School as a display aircraft. K3363 was part of the display team piloted by flying instructors. The upper wing markings allowing the crowds at the Hendon Displays to see that the aircraft was indeed upside down for many minutes on end.
Reference used: p19 'Spitfire, A Test Pilot's Story' by Jeffery Quill, Air Data Publications, 1996

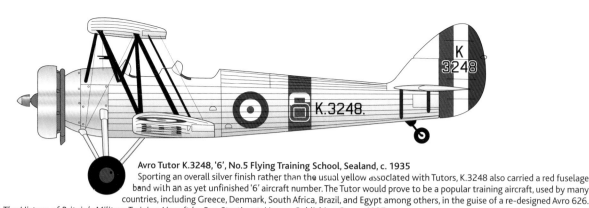

Avro Tutor K.3248, '6', No.5 Flying Training School, Sealand, c. 1935
Sporting an overall silver finish rather than the usual yellow associated with Tutors, K.3248 also carried a red fuselage band with an as yet unfinished '6' aircraft number. The Tutor would prove to be a popular training aircraft, used by many countries, including Greece, Denmark, South Africa, Brazil, and Egypt among others, in the guise of a re-designed Avro 626.
Reference used: p31 The History of Britain's Military Training Aircraft by Ray Sturtivant, Haynes Publishing Group 1987

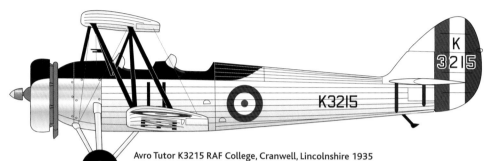

Avro Tutor K3215 RAF College, Cranwell, Lincolnshire 1935
K3215 is possibly the only surviving Tutor still flying, albeit under the serial K3241 as part of the Shuttleworth Collection. It first served with the RAF College, Cranwell between 1933-36 and then with the Central Flying School. It then went on to be used on communication duties during the 1940s before being struck off charge in December 1946. After featuring in the film 'Reach for the Sky' it was bought by the Shuttleworth Collection. Engine problems kept the aircraft grounded for long periods and it was after a lengthy re-build of the original Lynx engine that K3215 was finally restored to flying condition in 1982.
Reference used: http://www.edcoatescollection.com/ac6/Avro%20621%20Tutor%20K3215.html

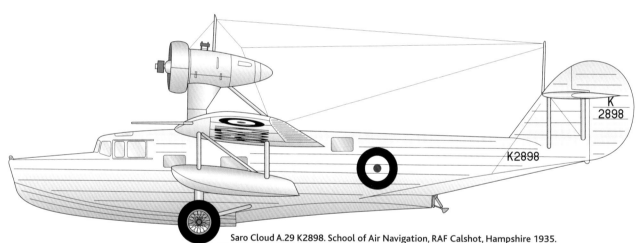

Saro Cloud A.29 K2898. School of Air Navigation, RAF Calshot, Hampshire 1935.
The A.29 Cloud was a military development of the popular civilian A.19 variant. It was conceived as a flying and navigational trainer. Its spacious interior allowed for numbers of students to be taught navigation simultaneously and its side-by-side dual control cockpit, ideal for pilot training. In 1932 the Air Ministry ordered 16 A.29s and these started to be received by the training units in August 1933 with production ceasing in January 1935. The Cloud was a true amphibian, being equally at home landing on runways with its retractable under-carriage as it was on water. It undoubtedly found a niche in the RAF performing essential training duties until being struck off in July 1939.
Reference used: p122 'Saunders and Saro Aircraft since 1917' by Peter London, Putnam 1988

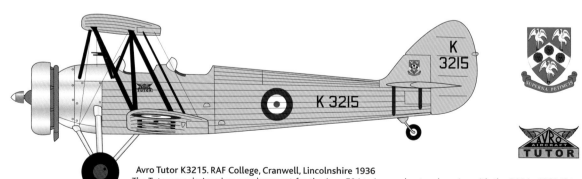

Avro Tutor K3215. RAF College, Cranwell, Lincolnshire 1936
The Tutor was designed as a replacement for the Avro 504 trainer and entered service with the RAF in 1933. Tutors from the Central Flying School became famous for their impressive formation aerobatic and inverted flying displays. K3215 was built as part of the RAF's main production batch in 1933. It is believed to have been the last Tutor on RAF strength when struck off in December 1946. Purchased by the Shuttleworth Collection it was restored to airworthy condition and K3215 is now the sole surviving example of the Avro Tutor worldwide. The aircraft is illustrated in its CFS livery, as it appeared for many years in the Shuttleworth Collection at Old Warden.
Reference used: from the private collection of Tim Walsh

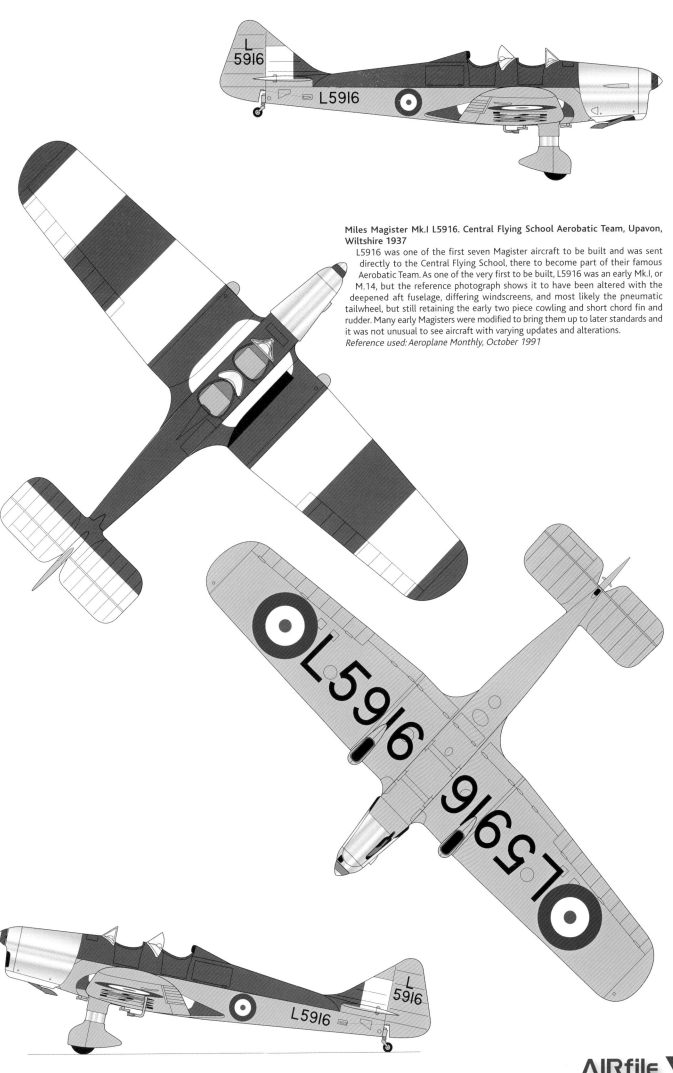

Miles Magister Mk.I L5916. Central Flying School Aerobatic Team, Upavon, Wiltshire 1937

L5916 was one of the first seven Magister aircraft to be built and was sent directly to the Central Flying School, there to become part of their famous Aerobatic Team. As one of the very first to be built, L5916 was an early Mk.I, or M.14, but the reference photograph shows it to have been altered with the deepened aft fuselage, differing windscreens, and most likely the pneumatic tailwheel, but still retaining the early two piece cowling and short chord fin and rudder. Many early Magisters were modified to bring them up to later standards and it was not unusual to see aircraft with varying updates and alterations.
Reference used: Aeroplane Monthly, October 1991

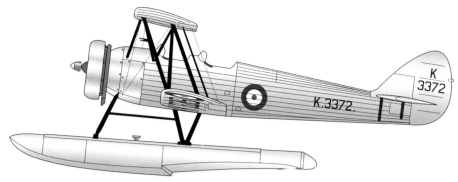

Avro Sea Tutor K3372. Seaplane Training Squadron, Calshot, Hampshire 1936
The Sea Tutor was a twin float seaplane version of the Tutor trainer. Fourteen aircraft in this specification were supplied to the RAF between 1934 and 1936. All were used by the Seaplane Training Squadron at Calshot to train flying boat and seaplane pilots. The squadron was comprised of four flights: - the Air Pilotage and Seaplane Training Flight, 'A' & 'B' Flights - Floatplane Training and 'C' Flight - Advanced and Night Flying and Navigation Flying Boat Training.
Reference used: p54 'Aircraft of the Royal Air Force since 1918' by Owen Thetford, Guild Publishing 1988

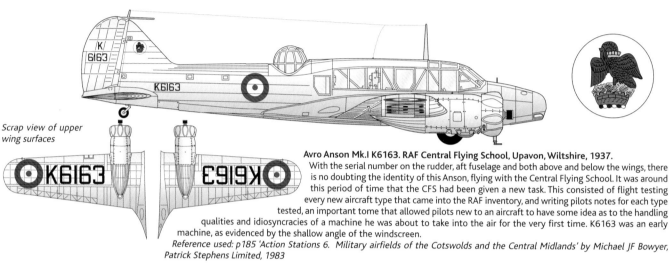

Scrap view of upper wing surfaces

Avro Anson Mk.I K6163. RAF Central Flying School, Upavon, Wiltshire, 1937.
With the serial number on the rudder, aft fuselage and both above and below the wings, there is no doubting the identity of this Anson, flying with the Central Flying School. It was around this period of time that the CFS had been given a new task. This consisted of flight testing every new aircraft type that came into the RAF inventory, and writing pilots notes for each type tested, an important tome that allowed pilots new to an aircraft to have some idea as to the handling qualities and idiosyncracies of a machine he was about to take into the air for the very first time. K6163 was an early machine, as evidenced by the shallow angle of the windscreen.
Reference used: p185 'Action Stations 6. Military airfields of the Cotswolds and the Central Midlands' by Michael JF Bowyer, Patrick Stephens Limited, 1983

De Havilland DH82A L-6923 '20'. Hatfield Reserve Flying School, 1938
With the outbreak of War becoming more and more obvious, the only question left to be answered was 'when'. As a result of the political climate, it was decided that the elementary flying schools be increased in number, with 50 eventually in existence by the time of the Declaration of War in September 1939. De Havilland had the distinction of being the first Reserve Flying School to exist (at Stag Lane in 1923), and moved to Hatfield in 1930. It was here that the first 1500 Tiger Moths in service before September 1939 were built and became part of the newly established Elementary and Reserve Flying Training School. At the beginning of September 1939 some of these Schools were disbanded and the remaining (20) were re-classified as Elementary Flying Training Schools.
Reference used: p8 'De Havilland Tiger Moth 1931-1945 (all marks) Owners' Workshop Manual' by Stephen Slater with assistance of the de Havilland Moth Club, Haynes Publishing 2009.

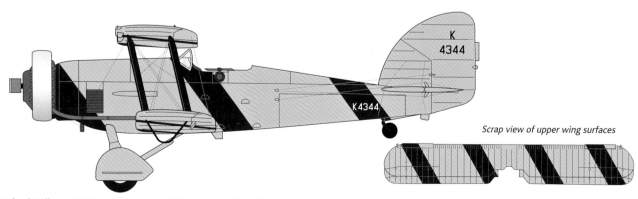

Scrap view of upper wing surfaces

Westland Wallace I K4344. No.1 Anti-Aircraft Co-operation Unit, Worthy Down, 1938.
K4344 was one of a number of elderly Wallaces that was converted for target towing duties. The aircraft began its career as Westland Wapiti K2313 which, along with over 60 other Wapitis were converted to Wallaces in the early 1930's. The black diagonal markings were 3 feet wide and placed 6 feet apart on both wings and fuselage. Reference shows no indication of roundels on the fuselage, but it is unknown whether it carried roundels on the upper and lower wing surfaces. K4344 was finally struck off charge in August 1943.
Reference used: p579 'Aircraft of the Royal Air Force since 1918' by Owen Thetford, Guild Publishing, London, 1987

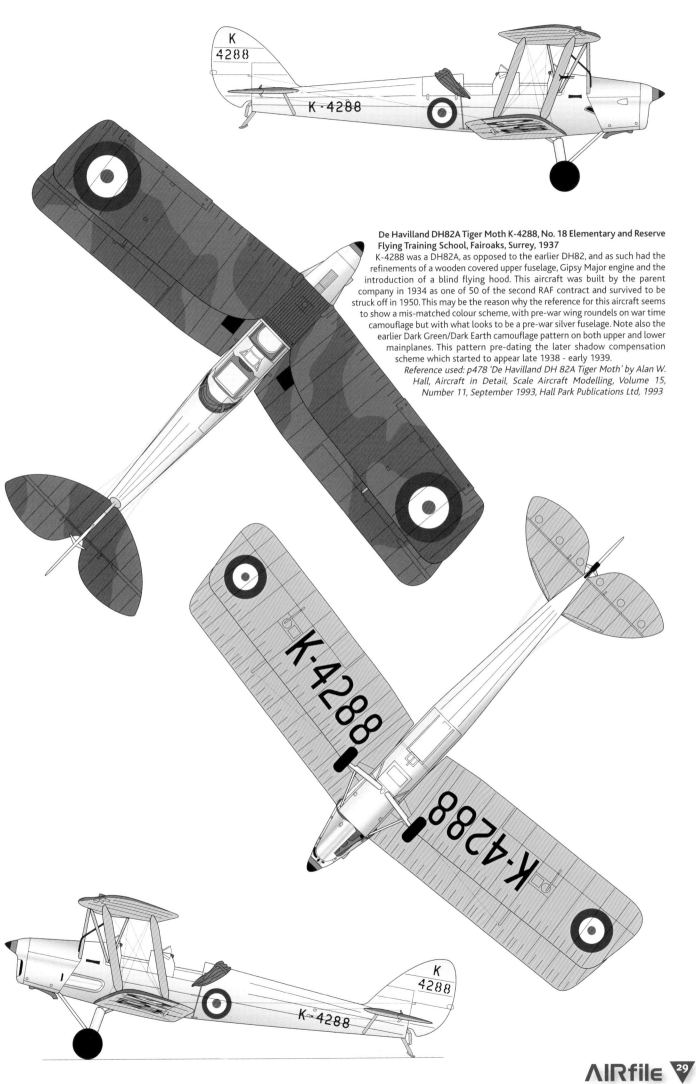

De Havilland DH82A Tiger Moth K-4288, No. 18 Elementary and Reserve Flying Training School, Fairoaks, Surrey, 1937

K-4288 was a DH82A, as opposed to the earlier DH82, and as such had the refinements of a wooden covered upper fuselage, Gipsy Major engine and the introduction of a blind flying hood. This aircraft was built by the parent company in 1934 as one of 50 of the second RAF contract and survived to be struck off in 1950. This may be the reason why the reference for this aircraft seems to show a mis-matched colour scheme, with pre-war wing roundels on war time camouflage but with what looks to be a pre-war silver fuselage. Note also the earlier Dark Green/Dark Earth camouflage pattern on both upper and lower mainplanes. This pattern pre-dating the later shadow compensation scheme which started to appear late 1938 - early 1939.

Reference used: p478 'De Havilland DH 82A Tiger Moth' by Alan W. Hall, Aircraft in Detail, Scale Aircraft Modelling, Volume 15, Number 11, September 1993, Hall Park Publications Ltd, 1993

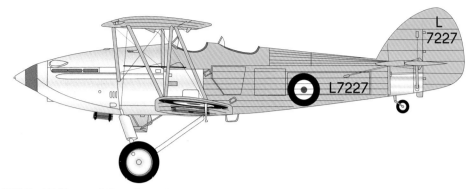

Hawker Hind Trainer L7227. No.610 (County of Chester) Squadron, RAF Hooton, Cheshire 1938
No.610 Squadron was formed in February 1936 at Hooton Park, Wirral, Cheshire as one of the Auxiliary Air Force Squadrons, equipped with Hawker Hart light bombers. As war approached, it was upgraded to Hawker Hinds in May 1938. In addition, there was a Training Flight for the instruction of Auxiliary pilots in dual control aircraft - a Hind Trainer, two Avro Tutors and a Tiger Moth. At first, the Squadron was manned entirely by regular RAF officers, NCOs and airmen. As the Auxiliaries were trained and became qualified in their flying and ground duties, they gradually replaced most of the regulars with the exception of the senior NCOs and instructors. In total, 139 Hinds were converted from the light bomber version and the last 20 aircraft produced were specifically built as trainers.
Reference used: p199 'Aircraft of the Royal Air Force since 1918' by Owen Thetford, Guild Publishing London 1988

Scrap view of upper wing and tail surfaces

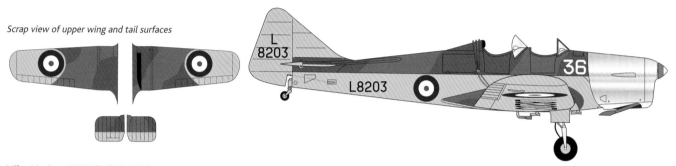

Miles Magister L8203 '36'. No.25 Elementary & Reserve Flying Training School, White Waltham, Berkshire 1938.
As Britain moved ever closer to War, the trainer yellow was soon to be replaced by much more drab camouflage colours. Aircraft that were down for servicing or repairs would have the new schemes applied, if the paint stocks were available, if the erks had the time and if they were of a mind to do it! Given the exigency of the time and the fact that new camouflage specifications were coming at a regular rate, it was not unusual to see aircraft with schemes that had been superceded many months before. The instructions for these colour changes could also be interpreted in widely (and wildly!) different ways. L8203 is a good example of non-conformity to the rules, with Dark Earth and Dark Green applied to the upper surfaces but omitting the highly polished cowl, and the wings were painted in such a way as to leave the roundels on a background of yellow, giving an almost wide-eyed, owl like countenance.
Reference used: Private Collection of Peter Green

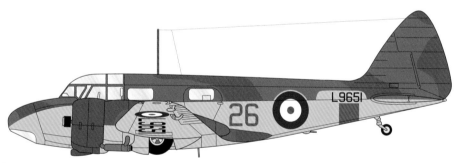

Airspeed Oxford I L9651 '26'. No.3 Flying Training School, South Cerney, Gloucestershire, 1939
L9651 was one of the second batch of 50 Oxfords built by Airspeed and was known as an 'advanced trainer', the earlier versions being 'intermediate trainers'. Popularly known as the 'Ox-box', it was regarded as a good trainer, in that it was necessary to give the aircraft the full attention of the pilot, and could quite easily give the trainee a fright if said attention wavered. L9651 was one of 400 serving with the RAF at the outbreak of War, and would soon be joined by another 8000+ examples. The aft red band and red fuselage numbers seemed to be particular to No.3 FTS at South Cerney.
Reference used: p58 'Yellow Belly - sidelines on a famous RAF twin-engined trainer' by Philip J R Moyes, Aircraft Illustrated, February 1969

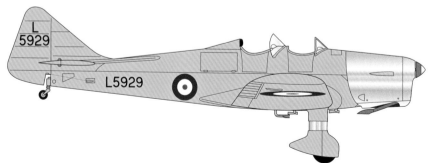

Miles Magister Mk.I L5929. No.30 Elementary & Reserve Flying Training School, Burnaston 1939
While the M.2 Hawk was a good aircraft, re-designing it into the M.14 Magister showed some shortcomings in the handling qualities, specifically spinning, and alterations were made to the airframe to alleviate this. An increase in the size of the cockpit areas to accomodate pilots with parachutes had changed the airflow characteristics over the tail area, the blind flying hood also contributing to the problems, so the rudder area was increased, strakes added to the aft fuselage and the fuselage itself was deepened. L5929 shows some but not all of these alterations, having the strakes fitted but retaining the smaller broad chord rudder and shallow aft fuselage. Other problematical points shown are the two piece cowlings and the tail wheel attached to the rudder post.
Reference used: p369 'Miles Military Trainers' by Alan W Hall, Scale Military Modelling, Volume 19 Number 8 October 1997, Guidelines Publications 1997

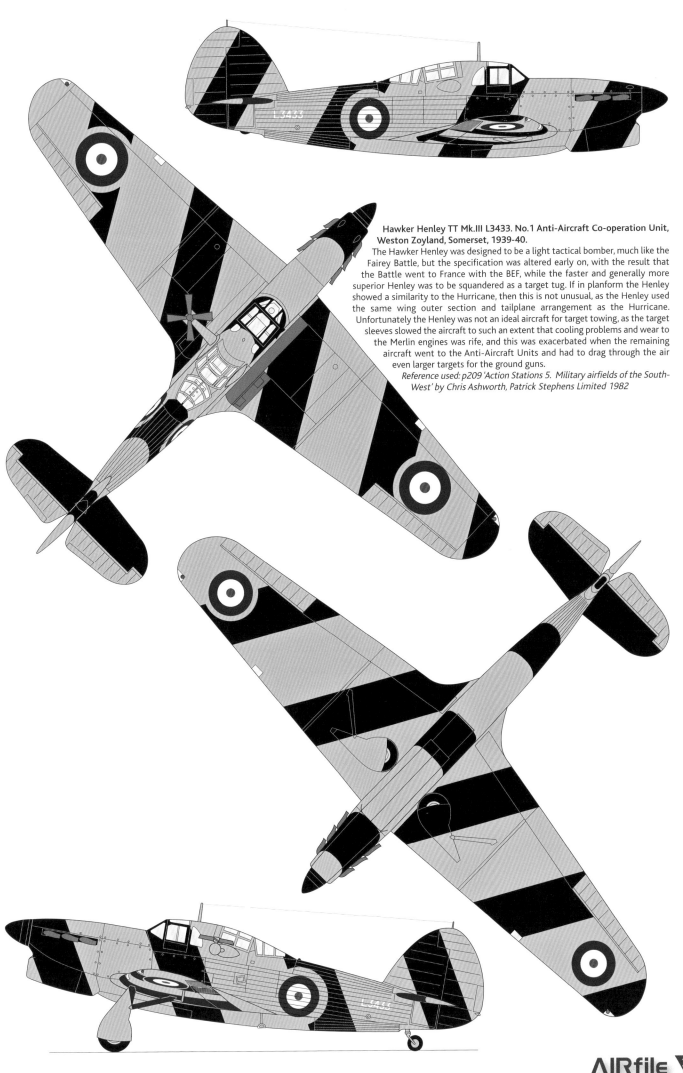

Hawker Henley TT Mk.III L3433. No.1 Anti-Aircraft Co-operation Unit, Weston Zoyland, Somerset, 1939-40.

The Hawker Henley was designed to be a light tactical bomber, much like the Fairey Battle, but the specification was altered early on, with the result that the Battle went to France with the BEF, while the faster and generally more superior Henley was to be squandered as a target tug. If in planform the Henley showed a similarity to the Hurricane, then this is not unusual, as the Henley used the same wing outer section and tailplane arrangement as the Hurricane. Unfortunately the Henley was not an ideal aircraft for target towing, as the target sleeves slowed the aircraft to such an extent that cooling problems and wear to the Merlin engines was rife, and this was exacerbated when the remaining aircraft went to the Anti-Aircraft Units and had to drag through the air even larger targets for the ground guns.

Reference used: p209 'Action Stations 5. Military airfields of the South-West' by Chris Ashworth, Patrick Stephens Limited 1982

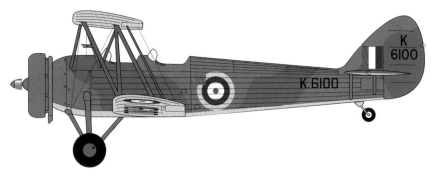

Avro Tutor K6100. Unit unknown 1939
The reference fo this aircraft definitely shows it wearing camouflage which will date the photograph as 1938/39. Other research has disclosed that many of the Royal Auxiliary Air Force squadrons, which were forming around this time, were using Avro Tutors. Also reference indicates that 310 (Czechoslovakia) Squadron trained on, amongst other aircraft, Avro Tutors - thus possibly dating the photograph as late as 1940/41. The authors welcome any further information that clarify K6100's history.
Reference used: httml://vintageaviation.michikusa.jp/poland_avro_621_1926.jpeg

Scrap view of upper wing surfaces

DH82 Tiger Moth G-ADGT 'GT'. No.6 Elementary Flying Training School, Sywell, Northampton 1939.
Sywell opened in 1928 as a civilian airfield and by 1935 was also operating as a military training field under contract to the Air Ministry. This military side was run by Brooklands Aviation using mainly Tiger Moths. G-ADGT was one of the aircraft used and is shown in the transitional period when camouflage was just being introduced. The pre-War overall yellow received a coat of Dark Green and Dark Earth to the top surfaces of the upper wing (and most likely Light Green and Light Earth to the top surface of the lower wing) and the upper part of the fuselage. The civilian codes were retained on the fuselage sides and under the lower wings and the last two identification letters were applied to the upper wingtips on large yellow panels. In later life this aircraft would become BB697, most likely with the camouflage scheme completed.
Reference used: from the collection of Mike Starmer

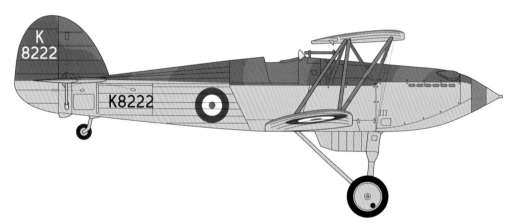

Hawker Fury I K8222. No.9 Flying Training School, Hullavington, Wiltshire 1939.
The Hawker Fury can be considered to be the ultimate in the single seat biplane fighter category, the clean, elegant lines of this aircraft thrilling the crowds at various air displays during the 1930's, pilots revelling in the power and precise handling qualities, the aircraft even being displayed in formation while tethered together, from take off to landing without ever breaking the streamers. K8222 is shown long after the glory days of silver wings, the shiny surfaces covered in drab camouflage colours and trainer yellow undersides, plying a new trade as an introduction to the newer types of aircraft coming into service. This aircraft unfortunately fatally crashed on the Long Newton range in June 1939.
Reference used: from the collection of Mike Starmer

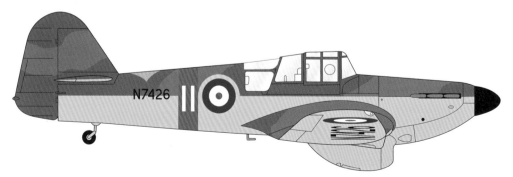

Miles Master IA N7426 '11'. No.5 Flying Training School, Tern Hill, Shropshire, 1939.
The Master looked like a fighter, was almost as fast as a contemporary fighter, and handled like a fighter, all of which stood the student pilots in good stead when they progressed to the Spitfire and Hurricane fighters. Indeed, provisions were made to create a back-up fighter from the Master by arming them with six .303 machine guns, and approximately 24 were converted to prove the concept, although fortunately, they were not called upon to prove themselves in actual combat. N7426 has yet to have a fin flash applied but has a red fuselage band with a white aircraft number. Colours and markings are otherwise standard for the period.
Reference used: p177 'Miles Aircraft since 1925' by Don L. Brown, Putnam & Company Ltd, 1970

Hawker Audax K7425. No.9 Service Flying Training Squadron, Hullavington, April 1940.

By 1939, the Audax had been relegated to mainly training duties within the redesignated name for the FTS of Service Flying Training Schools. These schools concentrated on intermediate and advanced levels of pilot training. RAF Camouflage colours had been undergoing consideration and testing since 1933. The camouflaging of aircraft began during the 'Munich Crisis' of 1938 and initially only top surfaces were treated with the Temperate Land Scheme colours. For biplanes this consisted of the four tone shadow compensating scheme of Dark Green and Dark Earth, and Light Green and Light Earth. Typical of changing periods of aircraft markings, K7425 carries some unusual styles. Note the demarcation line through the lower part of the fin, the position of the Gas patch close to the fin root on the upper decking, the absence of fin serial and the combination of bright pre-war fuselage roundels and the more recent dull red/blue upper wing roundels.

Reference used:
www.flickr.com/photos/16118167@NO4/51758991.24/in/photostream/

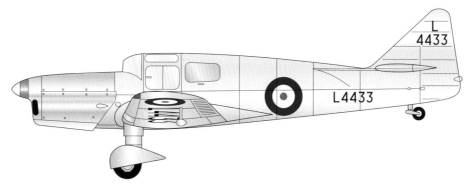

Miles M16 Mentor I L4433. Station Flight, RAF Manston, Kent 1939
Forty-five Mentors were supplied to the RAF between 1938-39 for radio instruction and communication duties. Eleven served with 24 Squadron on VIP transportation duties and the others went to Station Flights where the three-seat cabin monoplane provided day and night radio training and general communications duties. By 1950 all 45 aircraft had been retired or destroyed
Reference used: http://forum.keypublishing.com/showthread.php?t=107590

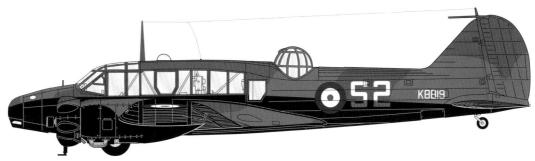

Avro Anson Mk.I K8819 '52'. No.1 School of Air Navigation, St. Athan, Vale of Glamorgan, Wales, 1939.
At the outbreak of War, No.1 School of Air Navigation were based at Manston. It was quickly realised that this was not an ideal base for a training school, and was rapidly despatched to South Wales. The period of occupancy by No.1 SoAN was short, for a year later it found itself in Canada, where it re-formed as No.31 Air Navigation School in Port Albert. K8819 is illustrated during the period the aircraft spent at St. Athan, still missing a tail fin flash but having had the undersides over-painted in black, possibly as a precautionary measure. The fuselage code shows up as white on the existing camouflage scheme and what appears to be red on the black.
Reference used: p79 'The History of Britain's Military Training Aircraft by Ray Sturtivant, Haynes Publishing Group 1987

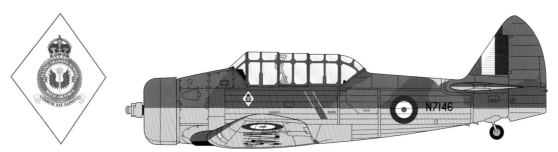

North American Harvard I N7146. No.2 Flying Training School, Brize Norton, Oxfordshire 1939
The North American Yale trainer was well liked by the British, so it made sense that they would want to buy the advanced trainer that followed the Yale. This was the Harvard Mk.I, which was basically an American Air Force BC-1 with British instrumentation and equipment. 400 Harvard Mk.I aircraft were ordered, in two batches of two hundred each. N7146 was from the first batch, and the aircraft from this 200 were unusual in that they all carried serials that were part of the U.S. Civil Registry system. Note the gas patch on the rear upper fuselage, a second patch was positioned on the port upper wing in view of the pilot. Also note the lack of yellow surround to the fuselage roundel.
Reference used: p112 'Aircraft Camouflage and Markings 1907-1954' by Bruce Robertson, Harleyford Publications Ltd 1956

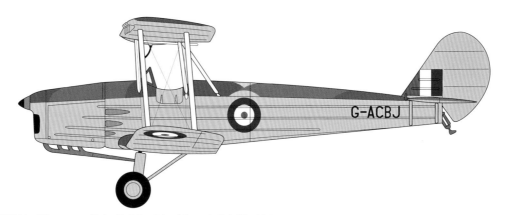

Blackburn B-2 G-ACBJ, No. 4 Elementary Flying Training School, Brough, Yorkshire 1940
Despite the plaudits and accolades afforded to the Blackburn B-2, only 42 of this metal clad trainer were built. In direct competition with the Tiger Moth, the B-2 never gained the popularity of the De Havilland product, selling none to any private individuals and no large order was forthcoming from the RAF. As a result the survivors, of which there were approximately 35, went to train pilots at the parent company's school, No. 4 Elementary Flying and Reserve Training School, at Brough from the mid to late 30's. This became No. 4 EFTS at the outbreak of War, and the B-2's still flying were given the standard trainer aircraft colour scheme, but continued to carry their civilian codes. Only the last three airframes of the production run were actually taken on to RAF books and given serials.
Reference used: p335 'Blackburn Aircraft since 1909' by AJ JAckson, Putnam & Company Ltd, 1968

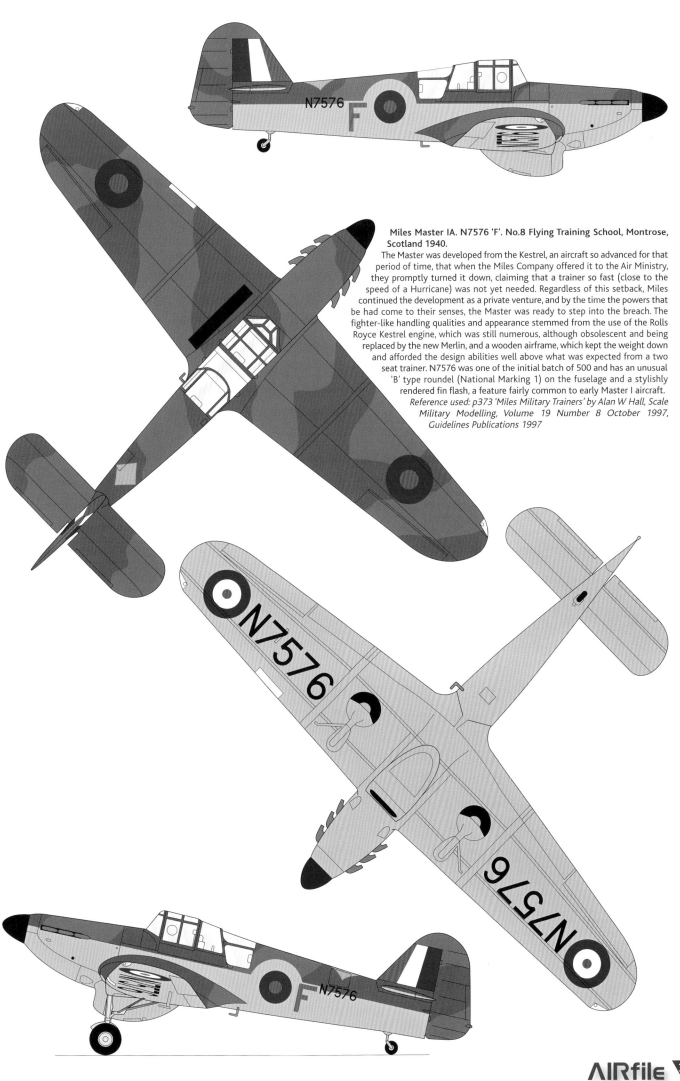

Miles Master IA. N7576 'F'. No.8 Flying Training School, Montrose, Scotland 1940.

The Master was developed from the Kestrel, an aircraft so advanced for that period of time, that when the Miles Company offered it to the Air Ministry, they promptly turned it down, claiming that a trainer so fast (close to the speed of a Hurricane) was not yet needed. Regardless of this setback, Miles continued the development as a private venture, and by the time the powers that be had come to their senses, the Master was ready to step into the breach. The fighter-like handling qualities and appearance stemmed from the use of the Rolls Royce Kestrel engine, which was still numerous, although obsolescent and being replaced by the new Merlin, and a wooden airframe, which kept the weight down and afforded the design abilities well above what was expected from a two seat trainer. N7576 was one of the initial batch of 500 and has an unusual 'B' type roundel (National Marking 1) on the fuselage and a stylishly rendered fin flash, a feature fairly common to early Master I aircraft.
Reference used: p373 'Miles Military Trainers' by Alan W Hall, Scale Military Modelling, Volume 19 Number 8 October 1997, Guidelines Publications 1997

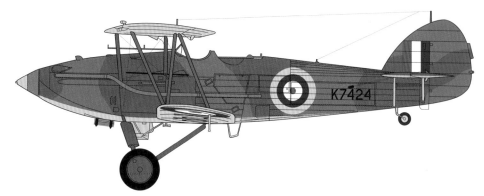

Hawker Audax K7424. No.1 Service Flying Training School, Netheravon, Wiltshire 1940.
K7424 carries full fuselage wartime camouflage, unlike many of its counterparts of this time which displayed the upper fuselage half camouflage and lower half trainer yellow. It was first delivered to the RAF College, Cranwell before being transferred to 1SFTS. Later it would see service with No.4 Glider Training School at Kidlington during 1942-43. Besides training RAF personnel, 1SFTS exclusively handled the training of Fleet Air Arm pilots and crew.
Reference used: p196 'The Hawker Hart Family' by Sue J Bushell, Aircraft in Detail, Scale Aircraft Modelling, Volume 15, Number 5, February 1993

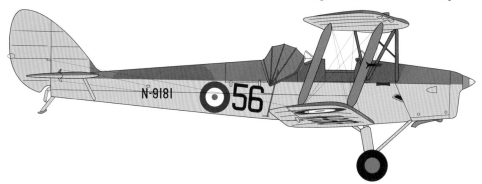

De Havilland DH82A Tiger Moth N-9181 '56'. No.10 Elementary Flying Training School, Yatesbury, April 1940
Regarded by the instructors who used them as a perfect training machine, due to the fact that it was an aircraft that tested and stretched the student pilot's abilities, while the students themselves sweated over the controls of a potentially difficult mount, especially when under the claustrophobic blind flying hood, as shown here on N-9181. This aircraft flew with 10 Elementary Flying Training School, which had been 10 Elementary and Reserve Flying Training School and run by the Bristol Aeroplane Company Limited prior to the outbreak of war. Noteworthy on this aircraft is the high camouflage demarcation line on the fuselage, lack of fin flash and the number 56 at a distinct angle.
Reference used: p27 'De Havilland Tiger Moth 1931-1945 (all marks) Owners' Workshop Manual' by Stephen Slater with assistance of the de Havilland Moth Club, Haynes Publishing 2009.

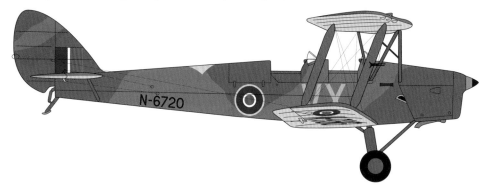

De Havilland DH82A Tiger Moth N-6720 VX 1939/1940 and present day
Tiger Moth N-6720 was, and is, a very rare aircraft, having taken on a combative role during the first part of the Second World War. This aircraft was one of a handful chosen to fly with one of the six Coastal Patrol Flights that were set up to deter U-Boats around the coast of Britain. Known as 'Scarecrow' flights, the idea was that an enemy submarine would not surface knowing that an aircraft was in the vicinity, even if it was just a Tiggy armed with a flare pistol and two pigeons! Still flying today, N-6720 has been restored to show the 1941 colour scheme, where the camouflage colours extend down to the bottom of the fuselage.
Reference used: p27 'De Havilland Tiger Moth 1931-1945 (all marks) Owners' Workshop Manual' by Stephen Slater with assistance of the de Havilland Moth Club, Haynes Publishing 2009.

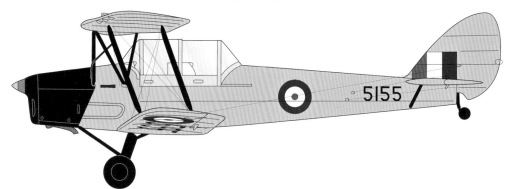

De Havilland DH82C Tiger Moth 5155. No.32 Elementary Flying Training School, Swift Current, Saskatchewan, Canada 1940
During the war a total of 2,751 Tiger Moths were built in Canada, Australia and New Zealand as part of the British Commonwealth Air Training Plan. The Canadian production Moths identified as DH82Cs had a sliding canopy, to compensate for their more extreme weather conditions. A hand braking system was also introduced and the undercarriage was raked further forward to provide more stability when learner pilots applied these brakes severely. A tail wheel was also added for taxying over rough ground. A number of Tiger Moths were also fitted with skis during the winter months and some with floats for operating from lakes. Actual production of DH82Cs began in late 1937 and a total of 1384 were operated during World War Two.
Reference used: from the collection of Mike Starmer

Fairey Battle Target Tug 1649 '6'. Unit unknown, Canada 1940.
Approximately half of all Battles produced were shipped overseas, 740 going to Canada, where they were used as target tugs, for gunnery training, pilot training and bombing training, and as such, were marked liberally with yellow paint over wings, tail and fuselage. While the early Merlin engines were lacking in power for such a large aircraft in a combat role, it was more than adequate for the training missions the Battle found itself fulfilling, a transitory mount between the Tiger Moths, Fleet Finches and such like, and the more combat ready types that the neophyte pilots would soon encounter. 1649 is boldly marked with the yellow and black bands that traditionally show that the aircraft is a target tow machine, one of 97 so converted.
Reference used: 'RAF Battle Camouflage and Markings' by Ian D Huntley, Scale Aviaion Modeller International, Volume 7, Issue 6

Hawker Hart Trainer K5861 '25'. No.7 Service Flying Training School, RAF Peterborough (Westwood), Cambridgeshire, 1940
Established in December 1935 at Peterborough, Hart Trainers, along with Tutors, Audaxes and Furies formed the nucleus of No.7 SFTS aircraft. Over 500 Hart Trainers were eventually produced and were used by many of the newly established training schools as the RAF quickly expanded its training programme through the late 1930's. No.7 SFTS service history abruptly changed in January 1941 when along with 13 other schools it was transferred to Canada as part of the Empire Training Plan, becoming No.31 SFTS, Kingston, Ontario.
Reference used: p13 RAF Flying Training and Support Units since 1912' by Ray Sturtivant with John Hamlin, Air-Britain (Historians) Ltd 2007

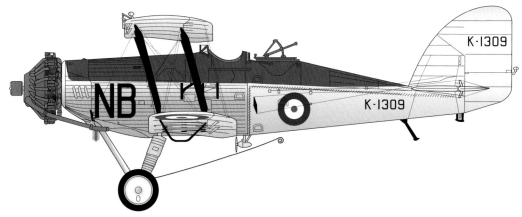

Westland Wapiti IIA K1309 'NB'. No.1 (Indian) Service Flying Training School, Ambala, India 1940
The Westland Wapiti was the sucessor to the DH9A in India. It was used for everything and anything and survived just about all that India's rugged terrain could throw at it. Flying in India as early as 1929, the Wapiti was destined for training and secondary defence duties by the outbreak of war in 1939. Naturally, it proved equally as useful in the training role. No.1 (Indian) SFTS was established in November 1940 to train predominantly Indian pilots. A wide variety of aircraft were utilised, especially in its early years including Harts, Audaxes and Tiger Moths. The unofficial squadron badge was of a Hawker Hart nosed over!
Reference used: p23 RAF Flying Training and Support Units since 1912' by Ray Sturtivant with John Hamlin, Air-Britain (Historians) Ltd 2007

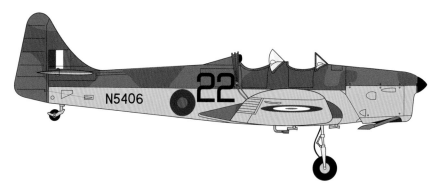

Miles Magister Mk.I N5406 '22'. No.15 Elementary Flying Training School, Redhill, Surrey, September 1940.
N5406 was photographed in a sorry state, having landed heavily and wiped off the undercarriage legs. The yellow fuselage sides would soon disappear after an Air Ministry order called for the colour demarcation line to be dropped to the bottom edge of the fuselage, this order starting to take effect from the beginning of 1941. The large number '22' in black (?) was a variation, one of many, in the positioning and colours of code numbers and letters and could be seen anywhere along the length of the fuselage. The overpainted fuselage roundel of dull red and blue contrasts sharply with the bright red and blue of the fin flash. Despite the damage to this aircraft, it was repaired and eventually found employment in Argentina.
Reference used: p6 'Miles Magister' by Michael Ovcacik & Karel Susa, 4+ Publication, Mark 1 Ltd, 2001

Scrap view of upper wing & tail surfaces

Miles Magister Mk.I P6377. 601 Squadron, Exeter, 1940
Pilot: Sgt Pilot Frank Jemsen
P6377 shows all of the recommended fixes that were necessary for the Magister to become an effective trainer. The engine cowling became a three panel structure, as opposed to the early two panels, which were found to be too flimsy, the tail wheel was moved forward and given a pneumatic tyre, the early ones of solid rubber not capable of withstanding the wear and tear, and the rudder is of increased height. The removal of the spats from the undercarriage legs was a normal practice, as most trainer airfields were grass and the spatted wheels had a tendency to collect mud and grass. By 1940, P6377 had become 601 Squadron's hack and Sergeant Pilot Jemsen had the unfortunate experience of writing off this Magister when it crashed near Colyford, East Devon.
Reference used: p14 'The Battle for Britain - RAF May to December 1940' by Paul Lucas, Camouflage & Markings No. 2, Scale Aircraft Monographs, Guideline Publications, 2000

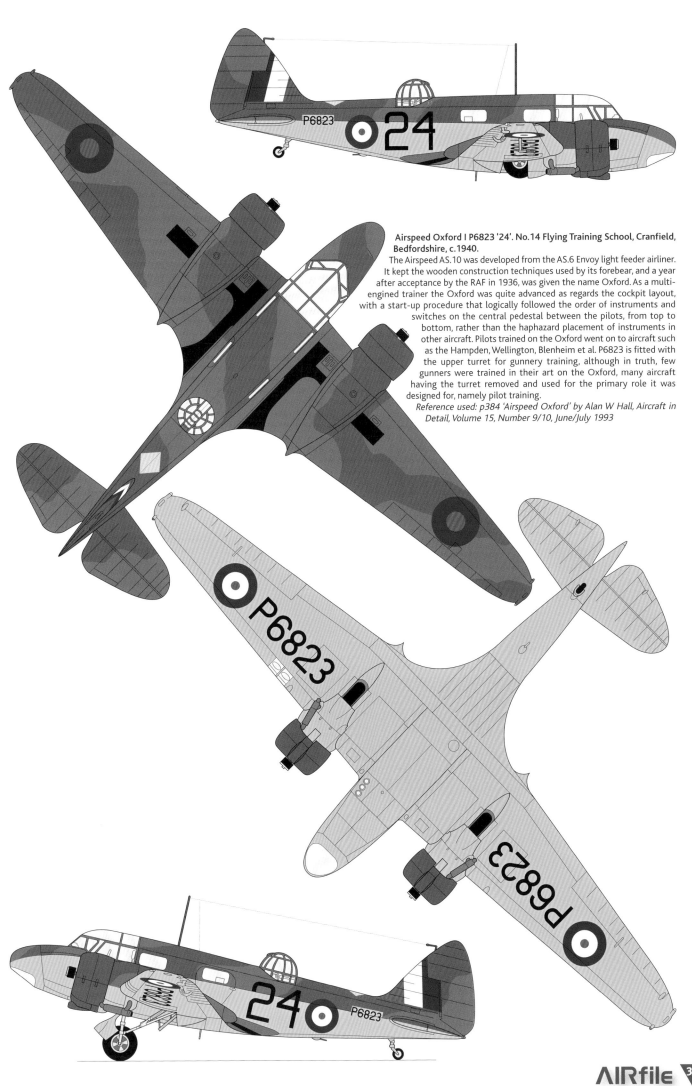

Airspeed Oxford I P6823 '24'. No.14 Flying Training School, Cranfield, Bedfordshire, c.1940.

The Airspeed AS.10 was developed from the AS.6 Envoy light feeder airliner. It kept the wooden construction techniques used by its forebear, and a year after acceptance by the RAF in 1936, was given the name Oxford. As a multi-engined trainer the Oxford was quite advanced as regards the cockpit layout, with a start-up procedure that logically followed the order of instruments and switches on the central pedestal between the pilots, from top to bottom, rather than the haphazard placement of instruments in other aircraft. Pilots trained on the Oxford went on to aircraft such as the Hampden, Wellington, Blenheim et al. P6823 is fitted with the upper turret for gunnery training, although in truth, few gunners were trained in their art on the Oxford, many aircraft having the turret removed and used for the primary role it was designed for, namely pilot training.

Reference used: p384 'Airspeed Oxford' by Alan W Hall, Aircraft in Detail, Volume 15, Number 9/10, June/July 1993

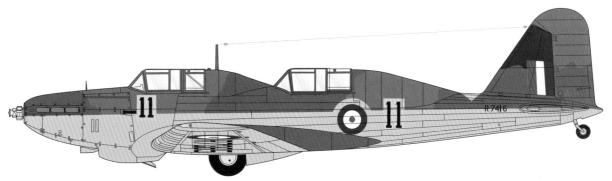

Fairey Battle Trainer R7416 '11'. No.31 Service Flying Training School, Collins Bay, nr. Kingston, Ontario, Canada 1940
No. 31 Service Flying Training School (SFTS) was the first British Service Flying Training school to be established in Canada. The school was originally No. 7 Service Flying School based in Peterborough, England. Some of the more noteworthy pilots who trained at No.31 SFTS were Lt. David Clarabut who earned a Distinguished Service Cross (DSC) for his role on the attack on the German battleship Tirpitz and Lt. Robert Hampton Gray, Canada's last Victoria Cross of the Second World War. Note the application of fresh Dark Green paint on the fin and freshly painted Ident. Yellow patches around numbers on the fueselage.
Reference used: from the collection of Mike Starmer

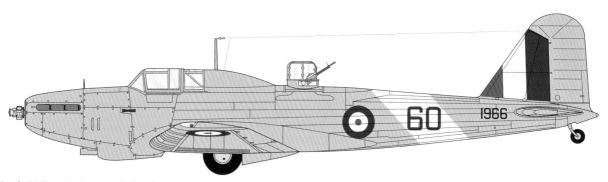

Fairey Battle T1. Turret Trainer 1966 '60'. Unknown Bombing & Gunnery School, Canada 1940
The Battle Turret Trainer was a conversion from a modification of the original Battle airframe. Several dual control aircraft were modified to take a Bristol Type I hydraulically operated turret for gunnery training purposes. 1966 was one of 202 converted to receive the turret, some, as mentioned, from dual control airframes, while others were converted from standard airframes. These performed dutifully until more capable aircraft such as the Bolingbroke began to take over the gunnery training. Even so, Battles continued to give good service right up to the end of hostilities.
Reference used: from the collection of Mike Starmer

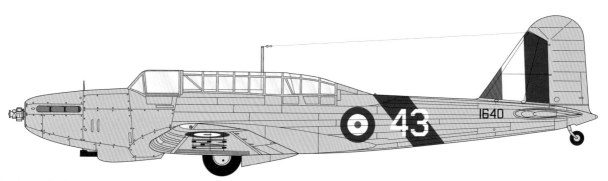

Fairey Battle 1640 '43'. No.1 Bombing & Gunnery School, Jarvis, Ontario, Canada 1940-41.
Battle 1640 was shipped directly to Canada from the U.K., and was part of the initial batch of 560 to be given Canadian serials. It is unlikely that the overall yellow scheme was applied before shipping, so this must have been applied some time after delivery, the monotone colour relieved by the standard markings and the fuselage decoration of a blue band overlaid with a white 43. Without any modifications, this Battle was kept as standard for bombing training. Normally the bombs on a Battle were carried in bays just outboard of the wheel wells, but the practice bombs used for training were attached externally under the wing on Light Stores Carriers.
Reference used: p9 'The Fairey Battle' by Phillip JR Moyes, Profile Publications Number 34, Profile Publications Ltd

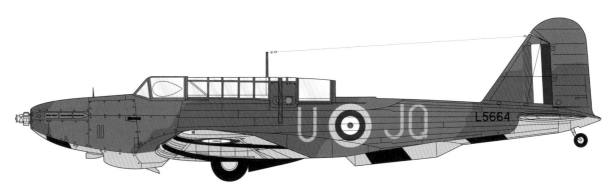

Fairey Battle TT L5664 'JQ-U'. No.2 Anti-Aircraft Co-operation Unit, Gosport, Hampshire 1940-41.
L5664 was built by Austin at Longbridge specifically as a target tug aircraft and unlike many Battles, stayed in the U.K. The rear gunner's station was altered to take the winch system, driven by the windmill attached to the port side of the canopy and was fitted with a drogue box on the underside of the aft fuselage. Unlike Canadian target tugs, camouflage was still de rigueur dress code on home shores and L5664 is coloured accordingly over the standard yellow and black stripes. Of note is the large blister to the side of the canopy, allowing the pilot a modicum of rearward vision, a feature seen only on British Battle target tugs.
Reference used: p63 RAF Flying Training and Support Units since 1912' by Ray Sturtivant with John Hamlin, Air-Britain (Historians) Ltd 2007

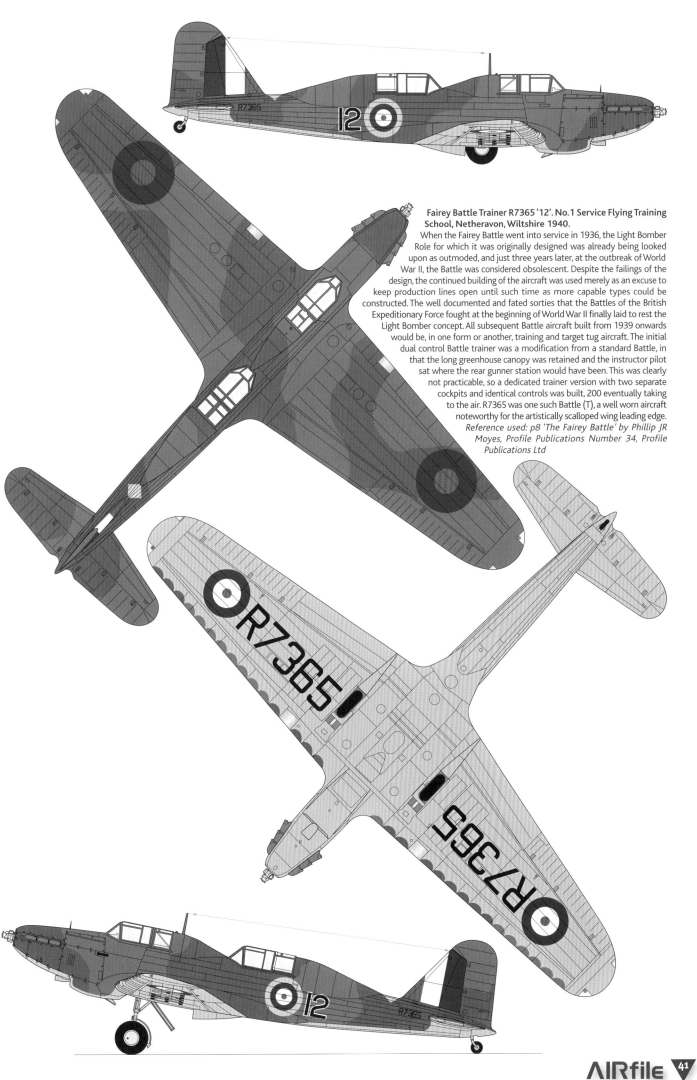

Fairey Battle Trainer R7365 '12'. No.1 Service Flying Training School, Netheravon, Wiltshire 1940.

When the Fairey Battle went into service in 1936, the Light Bomber Role for which it was originally designed was already being looked upon as outmoded, and just three years later, at the outbreak of World War II, the Battle was considered obsolescent. Despite the failings of the design, the continued building of the aircraft was used merely as an excuse to keep production lines open until such time as more capable types could be constructed. The well documented and fated sorties that the Battles of the British Expeditionary Force fought at the beginning of World War II finally laid to rest the Light Bomber concept. All subsequent Battle aircraft built from 1939 onwards would be, in one form or another, training and target tug aircraft. The initial dual control Battle trainer was a modification from a standard Battle, in that the long greenhouse canopy was retained and the instructor pilot sat where the rear gunner station would have been. This was clearly not practicable, so a dedicated trainer version with two separate cockpits and identical controls was built, 200 eventually taking to the air. R7365 was one such Battle (T), a well worn aircraft noteworthy for the artistically scalloped wing leading edge.
Reference used: p8 'The Fairey Battle' by Phillip JR Moyes, Profile Publications Number 34, Profile Publications Ltd

De Havilland DH82A Tiger Moth 2102 '36'. No.2 Air School, Randfontein, South Africa, mid-1940

The Empire Air Training Scheme was established by the British Government very early in the War to allow air personnel to be trained well away from the actual theatres of combat. Canada was obviously ideal for this, and while South Africa was invited to join the Scheme, it declined due to the comparatively close trouble the Italians were causing in Abyssinia. In December of 1939 this decision was reversed, to a certain extent, when all airfields and ground facilities were offered for training on the proviso that the British Government supplied all the aircraft and associated equipment. Thus was born the Joint Air Training Scheme. South Africa updated and improved all the airfields, which was no mean feat, while the U.K. attempted to provide the thousands of aircraft that would be needed. Tiger Moth 2102 was quite possibly a conscript from the civilian quarter, some numbers of these used to make up the requirements. As far as is known, No.2 Air School were the only ones to mark up their aircraft in this particular manner, with the School number on the top of the left wing, aircraft number to the right and to the front fuselage, and the serial to the aft fuselage and under the lower wings. Note the red doped repair patch on the rudder, a feature that was fairly common.
Reference used: p43 Yellow Wings by Captain Dave Becker, South African Air Force Museum Publications, 1989

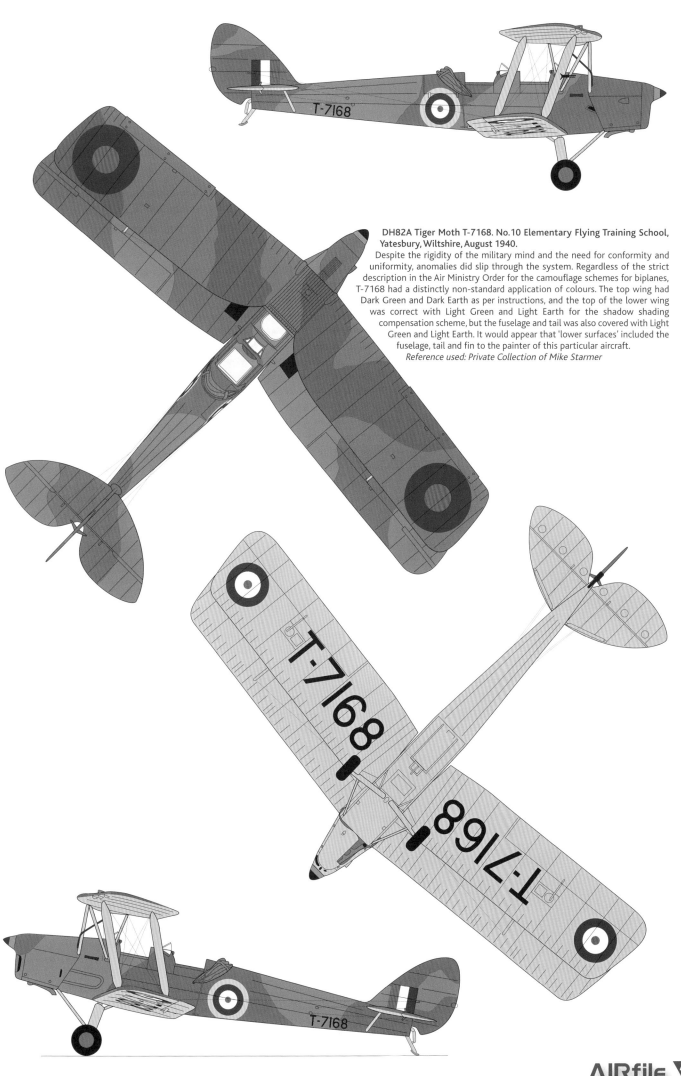

DH82A Tiger Moth T-7168. No.10 Elementary Flying Training School, Yatesbury, Wiltshire, August 1940.

Despite the rigidity of the military mind and the need for conformity and uniformity, anomalies did slip through the system. Regardless of the strict description in the Air Ministry Order for the camouflage schemes for biplanes, T-7168 had a distinctly non-standard application of colours. The top wing had Dark Green and Dark Earth as per instructions, and the top of the lower wing was correct with Light Green and Light Earth for the shadow shading compensation scheme, but the fuselage and tail was also covered with Light Green and Light Earth. It would appear that 'lower surfaces' included the fuselage, tail and fin to the painter of this particular aircraft.

Reference used: Private Collection of Mike Starmer

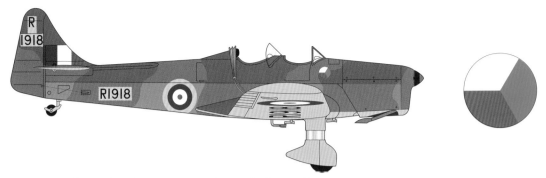

Miles Magister Mk.I R1918. 312 (Czechoslovak) Squadron, Ayr, Ayrshire, Scotland, September 1941.
312 Squadron was the second Czechoslovak Squadron to be formed (after 310) at Duxford and initially flew Hurricanes for one year, before going to Ayr to convert to Spitfires. R1918 was on strength with the Squadron at this time and shows the new camouflage scheme to good effect, with the serial numbers on the fuselage and rudder giving an inkling as to the previous scheme. The Czechoslovak roundel was displayed on all 312 Squadron aircraft, from the Hurricane to the Spitfire they would finish the War with. Underwing serials were not often seen on wartime Magisters, and the fin flash is of note, being the full width of the fin, as opposed to the usual equally spaced 8'' colours.
Reference used: p5 'Miles Magister' by Michael Ovcacik & Karel Susa, 4+ Publication, Mark 1 Ltd, 2001

De Havilland DH82A Tiger Moth N-6983 '52'. School and location unknown, c.1941
While most, if not all, of the Flying Schools in the U.K. were using Tiger Moths, it must be remembered that this ubiquitous aircraft also flew in the training role right across the globe, from the Canadian airfields, across India, South Rhodesia, South Africa, and all the way to Australia and New Zealand, tens of thousands of pilots, civilian as well as Air Force gained their wings on Tiger Moths. N-6983 has a completely standard colour scheme, relieved only by the gas warning patch on the aft fuselage and the number 52 on the fuselage side, the upper half of this outlined in white.
Reference used: p123 'De Havilland Tiger Moth 1931-1945 (all marks) Owners' Workshop Manual' by Stephen Slater with assistance of the de Havilland Moth Club, Haynes Publishing 2009.

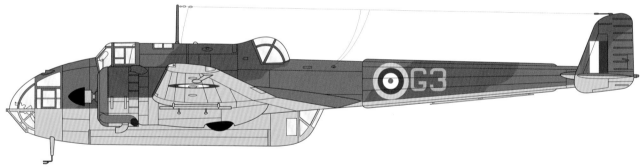

Handley Page Hampden B. Mk.I (serial unknown) 'G3'. No.5 Air Observer School, Jurby, Isle of Man 1941.
The Hampden, along with the Whitley and Wellington, formed the mainstay of Bomber Command at the start of the War. Despite appearances the Hampden was in the heavy bomber class, with an all-up weight of 21,000lbs. The early raids carried out during daylight were soon found to be suicidal, poor defensive armament and a lack of powered turrets meant that the aircraft was quickly reassigned to night bombing duties, where it had some considerable success laying mines. By September of 1942, when the last sorties were carried out, the Hampden was retired from bombing duties as the four engined heavies took over. Apart from the Meteorological Flights and a short dalliance with torpedoes, the rest of the Hampdens were used for training, both here and in Canada, 200 aircraft being ferried across the Atlantic. 'G3' was retained on home shores for training purposes.
Reference used: p8 'Handley-Page Hampden and Hereford' by Alan W Hall, Warpaint Series No 57, Warpaint Books Ltd

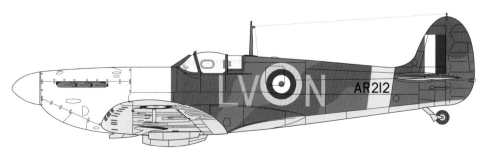

Supermarine Spitfire Mk.I AR212 'LV-N'. No.57 Operational Training Unit, Hawarden, Flintshire 1941.
Spitfire AR212 was a well used and well worn airframe by the time the reference photograph was taken. The freshly painted nose and spinner are in marked contrast to the rest of the aircraft, with chipping to the paintwork on the tail and dirt to the fuselage sides. By the end of 1941 AR212 had moved to 27 OTU, where it stayed until struck off charge in March of 1942. If the newly painted nose (yellow is also a possible colour) was meant to be highly visible, then in this respect it failed, as AR212 collided in mid air over Chester, coincidentally with a Spitfire from 57 OTU.
Reference used: p41 'Fighter Command 1939-45' by David Oliver, Harper Collins Publishers, 2000

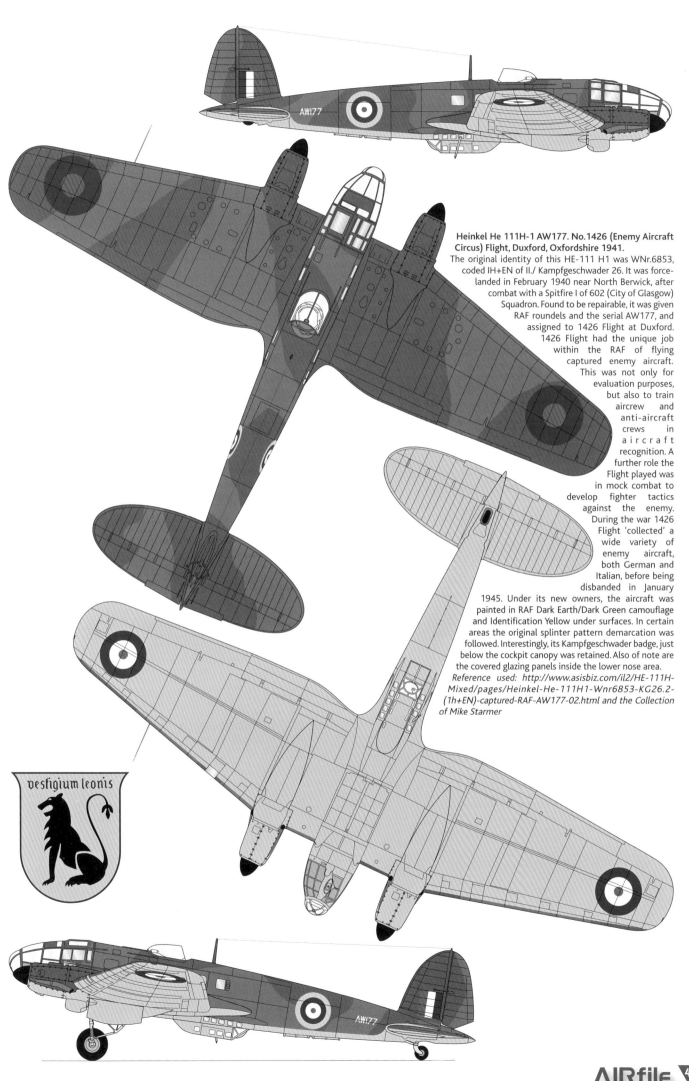

Heinkel He 111H-1 AW177. No.1426 (Enemy Aircraft Circus) Flight, Duxford, Oxfordshire 1941.
The original identity of this HE-111 H1 was WNr.6853, coded IH+EN of II./ Kampfgeschwader 26. It was force-landed in February 1940 near North Berwick, after combat with a Spitfire I of 602 (City of Glasgow) Squadron. Found to be repairable, it was given RAF roundels and the serial AW177, and assigned to 1426 Flight at Duxford. 1426 Flight had the unique job within the RAF of flying captured enemy aircraft. This was not only for evaluation purposes, but also to train aircrew and anti-aircraft crews in aircraft recognition. A further role the Flight played was in mock combat to develop fighter tactics against the enemy. During the war 1426 Flight 'collected' a wide variety of enemy aircraft, both German and Italian, before being disbanded in January 1945. Under its new owners, the aircraft was painted in RAF Dark Earth/Dark Green camouflage and Identification Yellow under surfaces. In certain areas the original splinter pattern demarcation was followed. Interestingly, its Kampfgeschwader badge, just below the cockpit canopy was retained. Also of note are the covered glazing panels inside the lower nose area.
Reference used: http://www.asisbiz.com/il2/HE-111H-Mixed/pages/Heinkel-He-111H1-Wnr6853-KG26.2-(1h+EN)-captured-RAF-AW177-02.html and the Collection of Mike Starmer

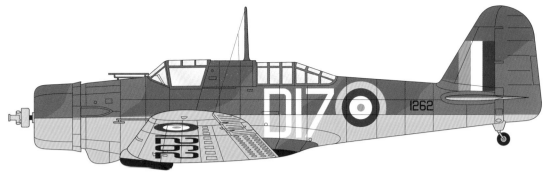

Northrop A17A Nomad Mk.I 1262? 'D17'. No.42 Air School, South End, Port Elizabeth, South Africa 1941.
By 1940 the USAAC had recognised that the Northrop A-17A was unsuitable for front line service. Sixty of these were dispatched to Great Britain under the 'lend-lease' scheme and subsequently 17 of these were allocated to training duties in South Africa. Referred to as just Northrops in South Africa, they became useful as target tugs. Fitted with a Grumman target towing winch, the Northrop could tow a 10 foot drogue for air-to-air firing exercises. Sadly, as spares were used up all were scrapped by 1944-45
Reference used: p96 Yellow Wings: The Story of the Joint Air Training Scheme in World War 2' by Capt. Dave Becker, SAAF Museum Publications, 1989

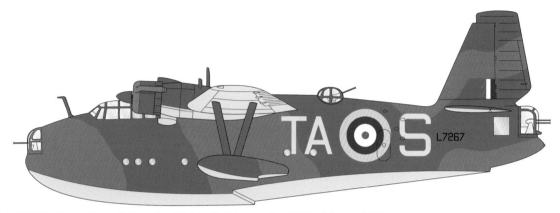

Saro Lerwick I L7267 'TA-S'. No.4 (Coastal) Operational Training Unit, Invergordon, Highland, Scotland 1941
The Saro Lerwick had a comparatively short service life with the RAF, only being operational between 1939 and 1942. It was intended to serve alongside the Short Sunderland in RAF Coastal Command, but it was a flawed design and only a small number were built. They had a poor service record and a high accident rate, for out of 21 aircraft, 10 were lost to accidents and one lost for unknown reasons. As a contemporary of the Sunderland it never proved up to the standards of its four-engined brother and was soon relegated to training duties. No.4 (Coastal) OTU provided Flying Boat crews for Coastal Command and was formed in March 1941. Equipped initially with Short Singapore IIIs, these were later supplemented with Stranraers, Catalinas and Lerwicks.
Reference used: p199 RAF Flying Training and Support Units since 1912' by Ray Sturtivant with John Hamlin, Air-Britain (Historians) Ltd 2007

Hawker Audax K7525. No.4 Flying Training School, Abu Sueir, Egypt 1941.
The Audax was developed from the Hart to replace the Armstrong Whitworth Atlas, the first Audax flying at the end of 1931. K7525 was built by the Bristol Aircraft Company, one of four manufacturers that were used as subcontractors by Hawker, 141 examples subsequently being constructed by Bristol at Filton. Before flying with No.4 FTS, K7525 was on strength with 52 Squadron and is typical of the second line equipment that was used in the Middle East. The reference photo shows a colour scheme that probably consists of Dark Earth and Middle Stone over Yellow. Note also the cooling holes in the upper cowl.
Reference used: p24 'Royal Air Force Handbook 1939-1945' by Chaz Bowyer, Ian Allan Ltd, 1984

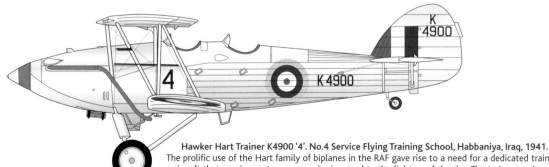

Hawker Hart Trainer K4900 '4'. No.4 Service Flying Training School, Habbaniya, Iraq, 1941.
The prolific use of the Hart family of biplanes in the RAF gave rise to a need for a dedicated trainer for an aircraft that was in most cases superior in speed to the fighters of the day. The trainer version of the Hart, with the aft cockpit area altered to accomodate a second set of controls, was the answer, with approximately 540 eventually being built. K4900 was one of 301 built by Armstrong Whitworth under contract, and is shown as it would have appeared at the time of the battle for Habbaniya airfield. Despite the dangerous circumstances which No.4 FTS found themselves in while defending the airfield and putting down an Iraqi rebellion, the 25 Hart trainers were found to be impossible to arm, and were used for nothing more than to make 'swoops and noises'.
Reference used: p75 The History of Britain's Military Training Aircraft by Ray Sturtivant, Haynes Publishing Group 1987

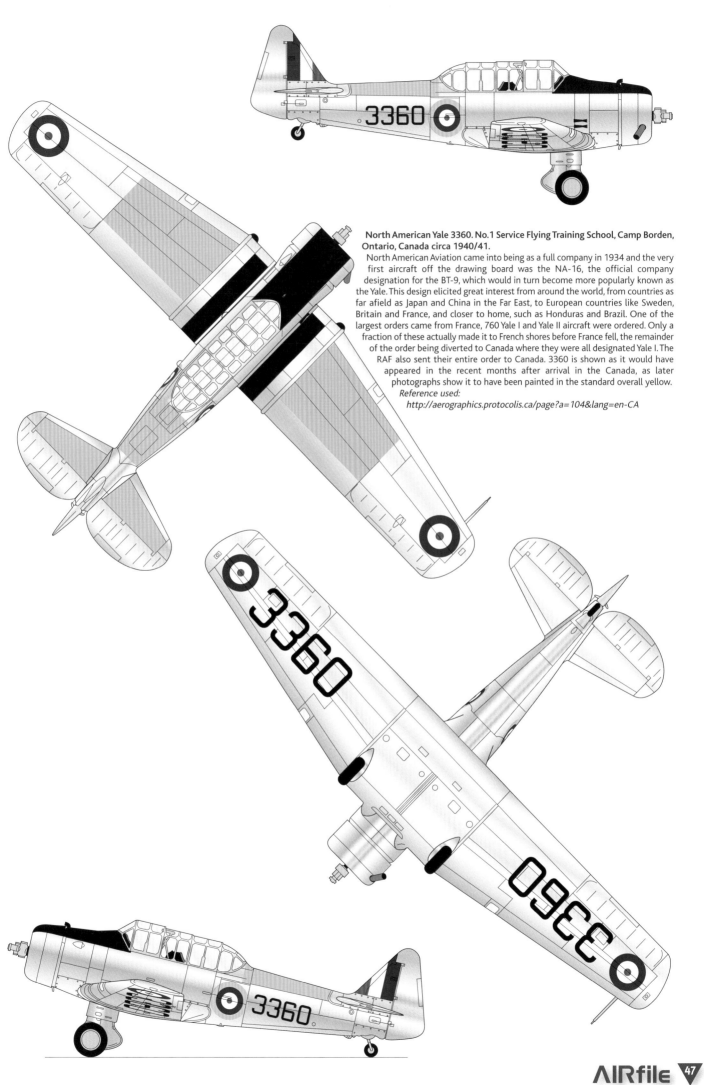

North American Yale 3360. No.1 Service Flying Training School, Camp Borden, Ontario, Canada circa 1940/41.

North American Aviation came into being as a full company in 1934 and the very first aircraft off the drawing board was the NA-16, the official company designation for the BT-9, which would in turn become more popularly known as the Yale. This design elicited great interest from around the world, from countries as far afield as Japan and China in the Far East, to European countries like Sweden, Britain and France, and closer to home, such as Honduras and Brazil. One of the largest orders came from France, 760 Yale I and Yale II aircraft were ordered. Only a fraction of these actually made it to French shores before France fell, the remainder of the order being diverted to Canada where they were all designated Yale I. The RAF also sent their entire order to Canada. 3360 is shown as it would have appeared in the recent months after arrival in the Canada, as later photographs show it to have been painted in the standard overall yellow.
Reference used:
  http://aerographics.protocolis.ca/page?a=104&lang=en-CA

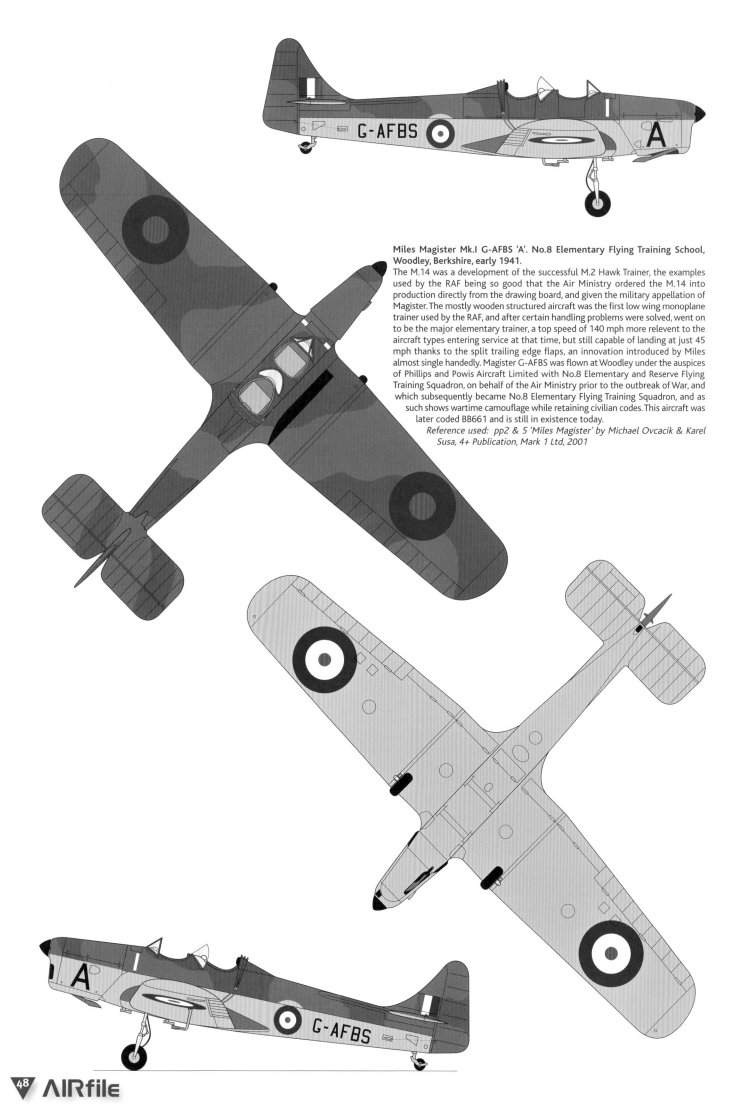

Miles Magister Mk.I G-AFBS 'A'. No.8 Elementary Flying Training School, Woodley, Berkshire, early 1941.

The M.14 was a development of the successful M.2 Hawk Trainer, the examples used by the RAF being so good that the Air Ministry ordered the M.14 into production directly from the drawing board, and given the military appellation of Magister. The mostly wooden structured aircraft was the first low wing monoplane trainer used by the RAF, and after certain handling problems were solved, went on to be the major elementary trainer, a top speed of 140 mph more relevent to the aircraft types entering service at that time, but still capable of landing at just 45 mph thanks to the split trailing edge flaps, an innovation introduced by Miles almost single handedly. Magister G-AFBS was flown at Woodley under the auspices of Phillips and Powis Aircraft Limited with No.8 Elementary and Reserve Flying Training Squadron, on behalf of the Air Ministry prior to the outbreak of War, and which subsequently became No.8 Elementary Flying Training Squadron, and as such shows wartime camouflage while retaining civilian codes. This aircraft was later coded BB661 and is still in existence today.

Reference used: pp2 & 5 'Miles Magister' by Michael Ovcacik & Karel Susa, 4+ Publication, Mark 1 Ltd, 2001

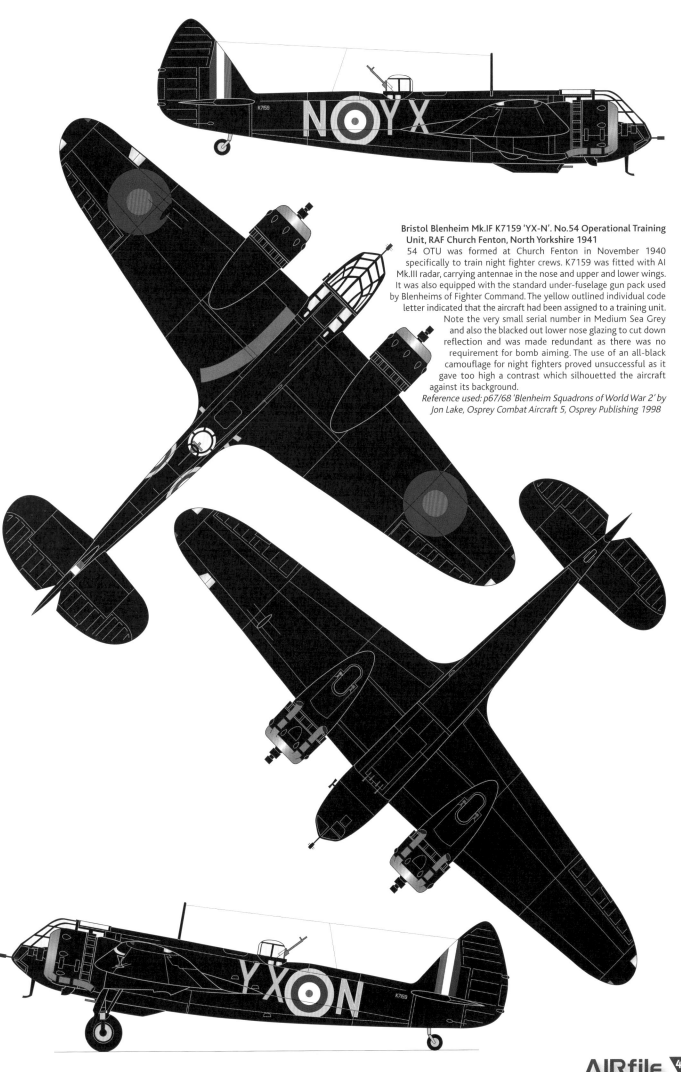

Bristol Blenheim Mk.IF K7159 'YX-N'. No.54 Operational Training Unit, RAF Church Fenton, North Yorkshire 1941

54 OTU was formed at Church Fenton in November 1940 specifically to train night fighter crews. K7159 was fitted with AI Mk.III radar, carrying antennae in the nose and upper and lower wings. It was also equipped with the standard under-fuselage gun pack used by Blenheims of Fighter Command. The yellow outlined individual code letter indicated that the aircraft had been assigned to a training unit. Note the very small serial number in Medium Sea Grey and also the blacked out lower nose glazing to cut down reflection and was made redundant as there was no requirement for bomb aiming. The use of an all-black camouflage for night fighters proved unsuccessful as it gave too high a contrast which silhouetted the aircraft against its background.

Reference used: p67/68 'Blenheim Squadrons of World War 2' by Jon Lake, Osprey Combat Aircraft 5, Osprey Publishing 1998

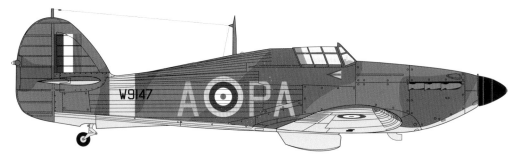

Hawker Hurricane Mk.I W9147 'PA-A'. No.55 Operational Training Unit, Usworth, County Durham, September 1941.
Pilot: Flt Sergeant Augustin Preucil
Hurricane I W9147 was delivered to the Germans by a defecting Czech pilot, Flight Sergeant Augustin Preucil who on a practice flight from R.A.F. Usworth, broke away from the exercise and landed at Ortho in Belgium near the Netherlands border on 18 September 1941. He was posted as missing and his aircraft was exhibited at the Museum for Transport and Technology, Berlin. Preucil had trained as a pilot in Czechoslovakia but became pro-Nazi and agreed to work for the Gestapo. As an agent, he first went to Poland in 1939 and then to France and eventually to Britain in 1940. His flying was deemed of mediocre quality and he was eventually posted to 55 OTU in 1941. In Britain he married but maintained contact with Germany and when opportunity presented, he defected to Belgium. In Prague he continued to work for the Gestapo occasionally as a Luftwaffe interrogator of captured Czech aircrew. He was eventually arrested on 19 May 1945, tried as a traitor and executed on 14 April 1947.
Reference used: 'Reported Missing' by R.C. Nesbit, Pen & Sword Publications 2009

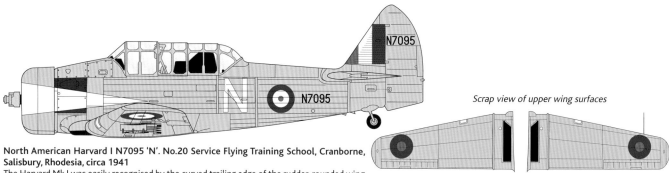

Scrap view of upper wing surfaces

North American Harvard I N7095 'N'. No.20 Service Flying Training School, Cranborne, Salisbury, Rhodesia, circa 1941
The Harvard Mk.I was easily recognised by the curved trailing edge of the rudder, rounded wing tips and a fabric covered fuselage. This latter feature was a deliberate attempt to use less aluminium, as there were fears that the bauxite used in the manufacture of this light metal could be compromised by the advances of the Axis Powers. These fears never came to pass and the later marks of Harvards were made entirely of aluminium. N7095 was from the initial 200 built and found itself part of the Rhodesian Air Training Group, with a smart white chevron to the nose and white code letter, both with a thin black outline. Note the blind flying hood in position in the rear cockpit.
Reference used: from the collection of Mike Starmer

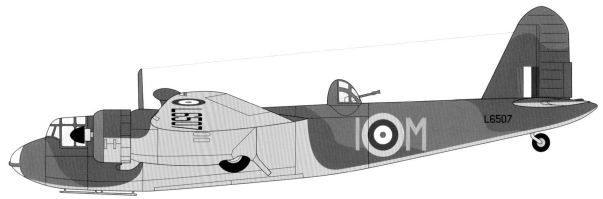

Blackburn Botha L6507 ' 1-M'. No.3 School of General Reconnaissance, Squires Gate, Blackpool, Lancashire 1941.
The Botha was not a successful aircraft in terms of operational abilities. Despite this 580 were built. A four seat aircraft with underpowered engines, it was envisaged before the outbreak of hostilities that it would be capable of filling the role of reconnaissance/bomber with an alternative role of torpedo bomber. The Botha failed to live up to these ambitions, only fully equipping a single Squadron, No. 608, and being used by them for a mere three months, from August to November 1940. It was after this brief operational foray that the Botha found its niche, being used by 21 various Schools, training aircrew in Bombing and Gunnery, Reconnaissance, Radio, Observation, Target Towing and Advanced Flying. Approximately 30 aircraft went to eight Technical Training Schools as instructional airframes. The Botha was declared obsolete in 1943 and the majority were scrapped soon after.
Reference used: p106 'Aircraft of the Royal Air Force since 1918' by Owen Thetford, published by Owen Thetford 1957

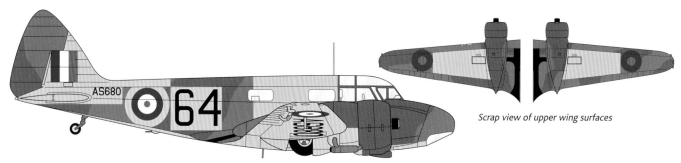

Scrap view of upper wing surfaces

Airspeed Oxford I AS680 '64'. No.35 Elementary Flying Training School, Neepawa, Manitoba, Canada 1942.
Once the Empire Air Training Scheme was established, it was not uncommon for aircraft to be shipped to the point of usage directly from the factories. AS680 was just such an aircraft, built by Airspeed in 1941 and going straight to Canada. With camouflage an unnecessary requirement, large areas of the airframe were covered with Trainer Yellow, resulting, as in this case, in a patchwork finish of camouflage and high visibility yellow. Eventually camouflage colours would disappear completely on indigenously produced aircraft such as the Anson, Bolingbroke and others to be replaced with an overall yellow, reminiscent of the pre-war RAF trainers.
Reference used: from the collection of Mike Starmer

Avro Anson Mk.I W2531. No.8 Service Flying Training School, Moncton, New Brunswick, Canada, September 1941.

Between 1940 and 1944, Moncton was home to the No. 8 Service Flying Training School, the No. 1 Wireless School, the No. 1 Y Depot, the No. 31 RAF Personnel Depot, the No. 18 Equipment Unit and the No. 15 Recruit Depot. The main aircraft used at the School were Harvards, Ansons and Mosquitos. Overall the training units based in the Commonwealth countries such as Canada and South Africa, carried far more colourful schemes and markings than their British counterparts. With no threat of hostile aircraft, the need for camouflage and dull colours was rarely seen unless on aircraft shipped over from the United Kingdom. Reference of this aircraft clearly shows the black markings running down the fuselage on to the wing fillets, but the shot angle hides any upper wing surface detail. Therefore, the upper wing markings are calculated interpretations only.

Reference used: p80 'The History of Britain's Military Training Aircraft' by Ray Sturtivant, Haynes Publishing Group 1987

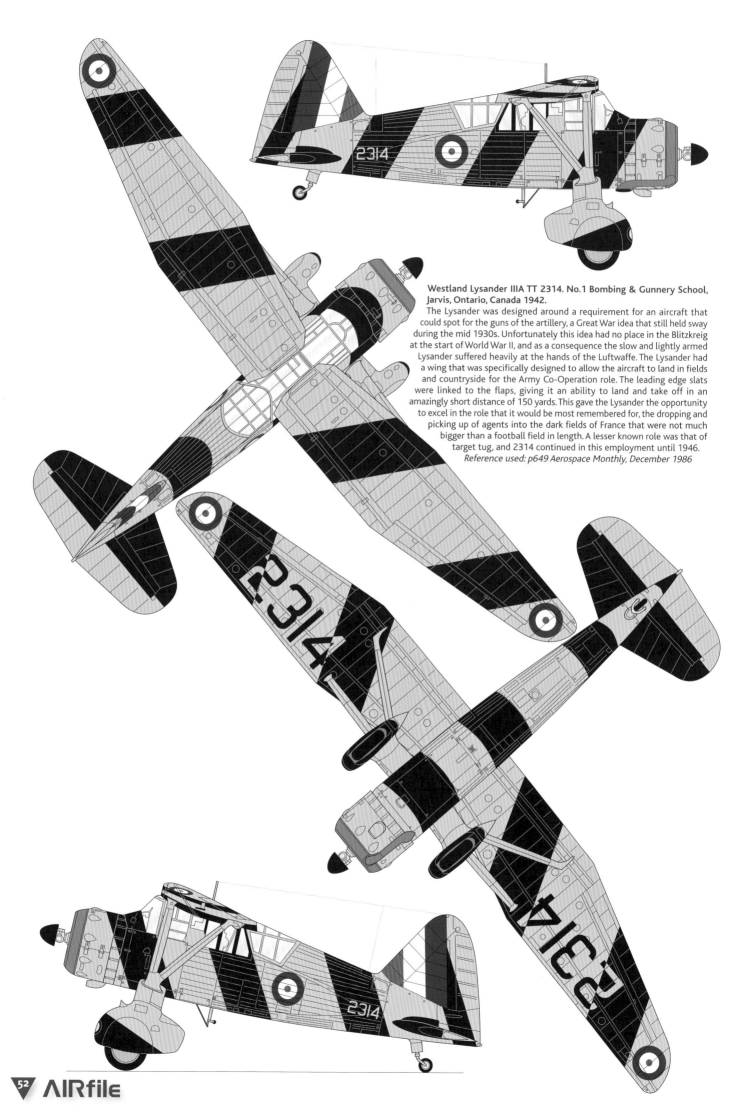

Westland Lysander IIIA TT 2314. No.1 Bombing & Gunnery School, Jarvis, Ontario, Canada 1942.

The Lysander was designed around a requirement for an aircraft that could spot for the guns of the artillery, a Great War idea that still held sway during the mid 1930s. Unfortunately this idea had no place in the Blitzkreig at the start of World War II, and as a consequence the slow and lightly armed Lysander suffered heavily at the hands of the Luftwaffe. The Lysander had a wing that was specifically designed to allow the aircraft to land in fields and countryside for the Army Co-Operation role. The leading edge slats were linked to the flaps, giving it an ability to land and take off in an amazingly short distance of 150 yards. This gave the Lysander the opportunity to excel in the role that it would be most remembered for, the dropping and picking up of agents into the dark fields of France that were not much bigger than a football field in length. A lesser known role was that of target tug, and 2314 continued in this employment until 1946.

Reference used: p649 Aerospace Monthly, December 1986

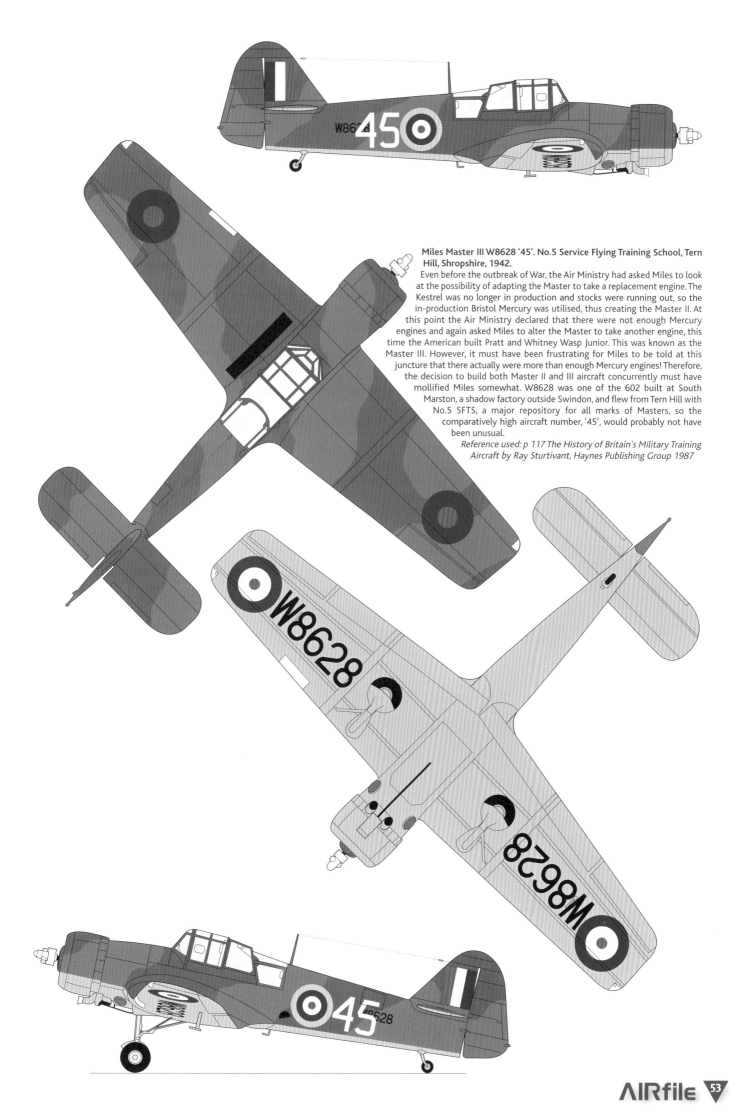

Miles Master III W8628 '45'. No.5 Service Flying Training School, Tern Hill, Shropshire, 1942.

Even before the outbreak of War, the Air Ministry had asked Miles to look at the possibility of adapting the Master to take a replacement engine. The Kestrel was no longer in production and stocks were running out, so the in-production Bristol Mercury was utilised, thus creating the Master II. At this point the Air Ministry declared that there were not enough Mercury engines and again asked Miles to alter the Master to take another engine, this time the American built Pratt and Whitney Wasp Junior. This was known as the Master III. However, it must have been frustrating for Miles to be told at this juncture that there actually were more than enough Mercury engines! Therefore, the decision to build both Master II and III aircraft concurrently must have mollified Miles somewhat. W8628 was one of the 602 built at South Marston, a shadow factory outside Swindon, and flew from Tern Hill with No.5 SFTS, a major repository for all marks of Masters, so the comparatively high aircraft number, '45', would probably not have been unusual.

Reference used: p 117 The History of Britain's Military Training Aircraft by Ray Sturtivant, Haynes Publishing Group 1987

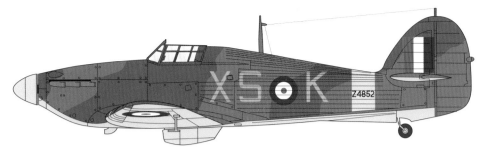

Hawker Hurricane I Z4852 'XS-K'. Merchant Ship Fighter Unit, Dartmouth, Nova Scotia, Canada 1942.
Formed at Speke in 1941, the unit provided aircraft for CAM-ships. The main type employed was the Sea Hurricane. However a small training establishment of 3 Hurricane Is and 2 Sea Hurricanes was also set up to provide pilots with catapult launch and maritime combat experience. Bases were established at Nova Scotia, Archangel and later Gibraltar.
Reference used: from the collection of Mike Starmer

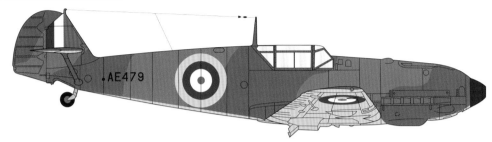

Messerschmitt Bf109E-3 AE479. No.1426 (Enemy Aircraft Circus) Flight, Duxford, Cambridgeshire 1942.
This early production Me 109E-3 (W.Nr 1304) was originally 'White 1' of 1/JG54 and was piloted by Feldwebel Karl Hier. He accidentally landed at Woerth near Bas-Rhin on the French border on 22 November 1939 due to fog. The French flew it to their Test Centre at Bricy near Orleans and, carrying French markings, it was test flown there then handed to the RAF on 2 May 1940 and flown to Boscombe Down under escort. After testing there it went to Farnborough for repainting in British colours and for more trials with the A.F.D.U. and later to Duxford and 1426 Flight. The Flight's role was to fly a variety of enemy aircraft around the UK for training in aircraft recognition and fighter tactics exercises.
Reference used: Aircraft Monthly, February 1986

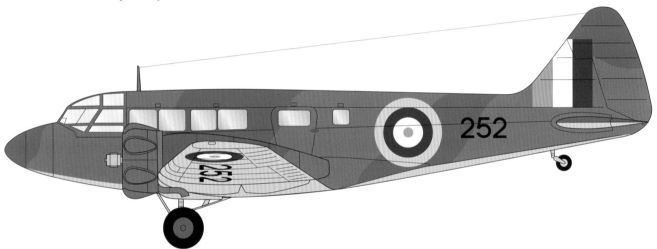

Airspeed Envoy '252'. No.67 Air School, Zwartkop Air Station, South Africa 1942.
No.67 Air School's primary role was photography and photographic training, providing courses at initial, advanced and instructor levels, but also training personnel to undertake survey operations. The school was established in November 1940 and initially operated DH Dragons, Envoys and curiously a Gloster AS.31. These were eventually all replaced by Avro Ansons. The Envoy while becoming a popular civilian aircraft, saw only limited service with the RAF in Great Britain. However it was exported to many overseas airlines and the air forces of Spain, Japan, South Africa, Finland and China.
Reference used: p72 Yellow Wings: The Story of the Joint Air Training Scheme in World War 2' by Capt. Dave Becker, SAAF Museum Publications, 1989

Vultee BT-13A Valiant (serial unknown) 'B262'. No.6 British Flying Training School, Ponca City, Oklahoma, USA, circa 1942
No.6 BFTS was operated under contract to the RAF by Harold S Darr, then president of Braniff Airlines, and was known as the Darr School. Except for a nucleus of RAF staff, all the instructors, ground staff and supporting staff were American civilians. The RAF staff comprised the Commanding Officer, Administrative Officer and three or four other officers, and NCOs for armaments, signals and other specialist training, discipline and pay. Training was similar in all BFTSs and occupied 28 weeks with all training being carried out at the same base. The Vultee BT-13A was seen as the intermediary trainer between primary training on the Boeing Stearman and advanced training on the North American AT6.
Reference used: www.fuselagecodes.com/id63.html

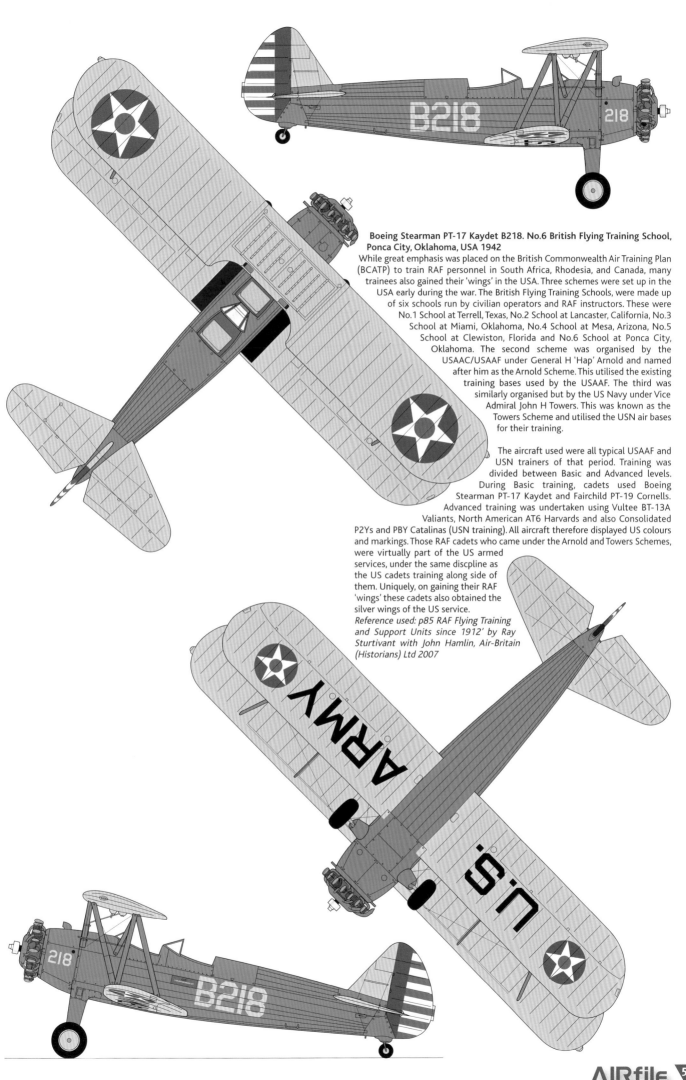

Boeing Stearman PT-17 Kaydet B218. No.6 British Flying Training School, Ponca City, Oklahoma, USA 1942

While great emphasis was placed on the British Commonwealth Air Training Plan (BCATP) to train RAF personnel in South Africa, Rhodesia, and Canada, many trainees also gained their 'wings' in the USA. Three schemes were set up in the USA early during the war. The British Flying Training Schools, were made up of six schools run by civilian operators and RAF instructors. These were No.1 School at Terrell, Texas, No.2 School at Lancaster, California, No.3 School at Miami, Oklahoma, No.4 School at Mesa, Arizona, No.5 School at Clewiston, Florida and No.6 School at Ponca City, Oklahoma. The second scheme was organised by the USAAC/USAAF under General H 'Hap' Arnold and named after him as the Arnold Scheme. This utilised the existing training bases used by the USAAF. The third was similarly organised but by the US Navy under Vice Admiral John H Towers. This was known as the Towers Scheme and utilised the USN air bases for their training.

The aircraft used were all typical USAAF and USN trainers of that period. Training was divided between Basic and Advanced levels. During Basic training, cadets used Boeing Stearman PT-17 Kaydet and Fairchild PT-19 Cornells. Advanced training was undertaken using Vultee BT-13A Valiants, North American AT6 Harvards and also Consolidated P2Ys and PBY Catalinas (USN training). All aircraft therefore displayed US colours and markings. Those RAF cadets who came under the Arnold and Towers Schemes, were virtually part of the US armed services, under the same discpline as the US cadets training along side of them. Uniquely, on gaining their RAF 'wings' these cadets also obtained the silver wings of the US service.

Reference used: p85 RAF Flying Training and Support Units since 1912' by Ray Sturtivant with John Hamlin, Air-Britain (Historians) Ltd 2007

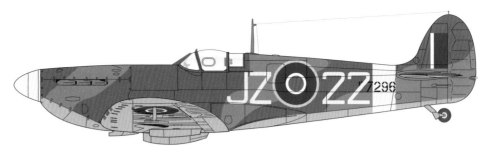

Supermarine Spitfire IIA P7296 'JZ-22'. No.57 Operational Training Unit, RAF Hawarden, Flintshire, Wales circa 1942
57 OTU was formed in November 1940 to train single-seat fighter crew using Spitfires and Miles Masters before being dispatched to operational squadrons. Plans were made in 1940 that would have made 57 OTU operational as 557 Squadron, moving them to Newcastle in the event of a German invasion. RAF Hawarden was close by the Vickers Armstrong shadow factory at Broughton and its aircraft also acted as an air defence unit if so required. During the Battle of Britain, such places as RAF Hawarden and RAF Sealand acted as 'rest' bases where depleted fighter squadrons could re-group.
Reference used: p207 'RAF Flying Training and Support Units since 1912' by Ray Sturtivant with John Hamlin, Air-Britain (Historians) Ltd 2007

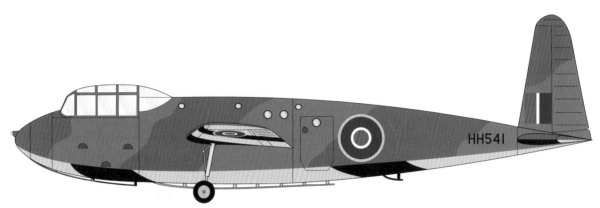

General Aircraft Hotspur II HH541 'Y1'. Glider Pilot Exercise Unit, Netheravon, Wiltshire, October 1942.
When the prototype Hotspur I flew at the beginning of November 1940, it became the first purpose built glider assault aircraft used by the Allies. This was developed into the Hotspur II, with a shorter wingspan (to allow for a much steeper approach angle to the landing site), and a side door large enough to permit parachute drops by the six men in the rear cabin. The front cabin was separated from the rear by the main spar, and accomodated the two pilots in tandem. The Hotspur never went into combat and was used exclusively for training purposes only.
Reference used: p94-5 'The Royal Air Force of World War Two in Colour' by Roger A Freeman, Arms and Armour Press 1993

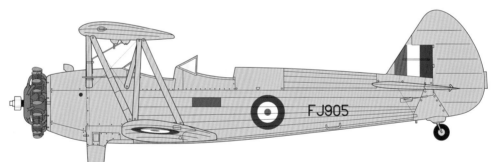

Boeing Stearman Kaydet I FJ905. No.32 Elementary Flying Training School, Bowden, Alberta, Canada 1942
The Stearman Kaydet can be considered to be the American equivalent of the Tiger Moth. FJ905 was one of 300 specifically built for the RAF (by way of the RCAF) under the designation of PT-27, which was essentially the same as the PT-17, an up-engined version of the original PT-13. An initial batch of 32 aircraft went to the Canadian Flying Schools. The second batch of 268 aircraft were retained in America on behalf of the RCAF with the exception of just 9 Kaydets, these being the only ones from this batch to go to Canada, and FJ905 was one of these aircraft sent North in 1942.
Reference used: p104 'RAF Flying Training and Support Units since 1912' by Ray Sturtivant with John Hamlin, Air-Britain (Historians) Ltd 2007

Cessna Crane 1A 7862. No.4 Service Flying Training School, Saskatoon, Saskatchewan, Canada 1942.
The Cessna T-50 Crane, or Bobcat as it was known in US service, was a light twin engine trainer procured in large numbers for both the RCAF and the US military during World War II. 822 T-50s were produced for the RCAF and became known as Crane 1s. A further 182 AT-17s (USAAC designation for the T-50 with modifications) were delivered to Canada under the lend-lease scheme and these were named Crane 1As. The aircraft was conventional for the period, featuring a low cantilever wing and being of a mixed material construction with the wings and tail being of wood and the fuselage being of welded steel tube. The Crane provided valuable multi-engine training throughout the war and supplemented the Avro Anson in the British Commonwealth Air Training Plan service. 7862 is one of a number of surviving Cessna Cranes and is currently exhibited at the Canadian Warplane Heritage Museum, Mount Hope, Canada.
Reference used: www.warplane.com/pages/aircraft_crane.html

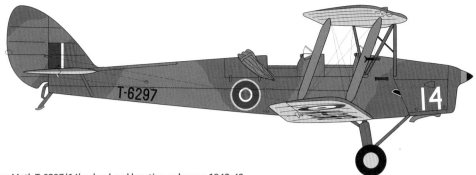

De Havilland DH82A Tiger Moth T-6297 '14', school and location unknown 1942-43
Apart from the white number 14 on the engine cowling, an otherwise anonymous T-6297 was one of the 8000 plus DH 82's built that fulfilled the day to day task of training the pilots that were to go on to fly the combat missions in the Second World War, and to continue after the War, the Tiger Moth not being retired from the RAF until 1951. T-6297 was built by Morris Motors Limited, which took over the main production run when De Havilland commenced making the Mosquito, 3508 Tiger Moths ultimately being built by Morris Motors. T-6297 clearly shows the late war colour scheme, with the camouflage taken completely down the fuselage sides.
Reference used: p78 'Per Ardua Ad Astra' by Michael Donne & Squadron Leader Cynthia Fowler, Frederick Muller Limited, 1982

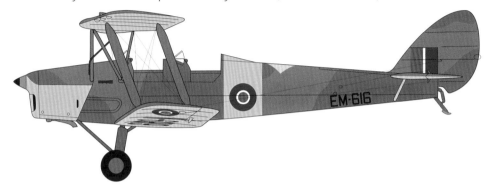

De Havilland DH82A Tiger Moth EM-616, 16 Elementary Flying Training School, Shoreham, 1943
The provision for the blind flying hood was built into every DH 82A Tiger Moth, so EM-616 must have been the exception to this rule, for the addition of a headrest must have precluded this facility. Yellow band and yellow cowl compromise an otherwise normal colour scheme. It was the repeated painting of the airframe combined with the aileron mass balances and the addition of bomb racks that caused the aircraft to start to have problems with spinning and this led to the addition of anti-spin strakes to the fuselage just in front of the tail unit. Many of the aircraft flying today still carry this modification.
Reference used: p480 'De Havilland DH82A Tiger Moth' by Alan W Hall, Aircraft in Detail, Scale Aricraft Modelling, Volume 15, Number 11, September 1993, Hall Park Publications Ltd, 1993

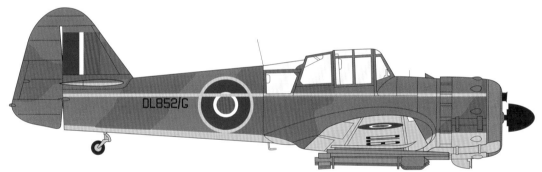

Miles Master II DL852/G. Aeroplane & Armament Experimental/Evaluation Establishment (A&AEE), Boscombe Down, 1943.
Replacement of the in-line engine with a radial engine on the Master II, meant that the forward view was compromised to a certain extent, but this was offset against the fact that the Mercury engine had more horsepower, giving the Master II a speed increase of 16mph, despite the greater frontal area. DL852/G is shown as a trainer with teeth, carrying six rocket projectiles, although it was only used as a test bed. Testing for this weapon was carried out, as was usual, at Boscombe Down and apart from the standard colouring and markings, DL852/G has a yellow line along the fuselage which was probably used as a datum line for photographic purposes and a 'G' suffix to the serial number, indicating that the aircraft had to be under armed guard at all times while on the ground, as the rockets were still secret at this time.
Reference used: p374 'Miles Military Trainers' by Alan W Hall, Scale Military Modelling, Volume 19 Number 8 October 1997, Guidelines Publications 1997

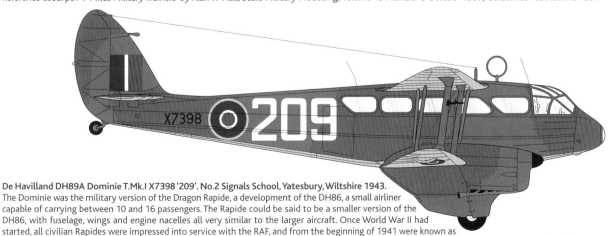

De Havilland DH89A Dominie T.Mk.I X7398 '209'. No.2 Signals School, Yatesbury, Wiltshire 1943.
The Dominie was the military version of the Dragon Rapide, a development of the DH86, a small airliner capable of carrying between 10 and 16 passengers. The Rapide could be said to be a smaller version of the DH86, with fuselage, wings and engine nacelles all very similar to the larger aircraft. Once World War II had started, all civilian Rapides were impressed into service with the RAF, and from the beginning of 1941 were known as Dominies. There were two versions, the Mk.II, which was used for transport and communications work, and the Mk.I, used as a navigation and wireless trainer, and was easily distinguished from the former by the large DF loop on the fuselage top. X7398 was built at Hatfield as part of an RAF contract, and not an impressed airframe, and was heavily employed in the training of Wireless Operators and Navigators at Yatesbury, which was the centre for RAF and WAAF personnel, many thousands being trained there.
Reference used: p104 'De Havilland DH.89A Dragon Rapide' by Alan W Hall, Aircraft in Detail, Scale Aircraft Modelling, Volume 14, Number 3, December 1991

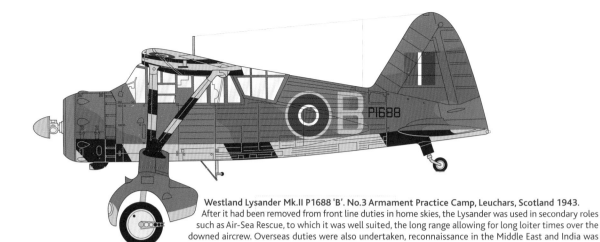

Westland Lysander Mk.II P1688 'B'. No.3 Armament Practice Camp, Leuchars, Scotland 1943.
After it had been removed from front line duties in home skies, the Lysander was used in secondary roles such as Air-Sea Rescue, to which it was well suited, the long range allowing for long loiter times over the downed aircrew. Overseas duties were also undertaken, reconnaissance in the Middle East and India was possible while ever adequate fighter cover was available. Target towing was also an obvious choice for an aircraft that could fly as slow and as stable as the Lysander. P1688 has a standard colour scheme, above and below, as per regulations.
Reference used: p56 'The Long Drag - A Short History of British Target Towing' by Don Evans, Flight Recorder Publications 2004

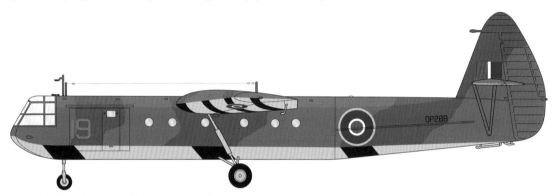

Airspeed Horsa I DP288 '19'. No.21 Heavy Glider Conversion Unit, Brize Norton, Oxfordshire, June 1943.
The smaller Hotspur assault glider was used basically to prove the concept of attacking a chosen site by glider but was patently not large enough to carry sufficient troops to guarantee the success of such an operation. The Horsa was a much larger aircraft, capable of transporting 25 troops and two pilots, and later versions were to carry Bren Carriers, jeeps, motorcycles and howitzers. DP288 was an early Mark I, used for paratroop training only and carried the standard black and yellow underside stripes, but the upper surface colours are noteworthy, where the Dark Earth and Dark Green have been extended down the black fuselage sides, the fresh paint contrasting with the earlier older paint.
Reference used: p95 'The Royal Air Force of World War Two in Colour' by Roger A Freeman, Arms & Armour Press, 1993 and p278 'Horsa Glider Colours' by Les Whitehouse, Scale Models Magazine, June 1976

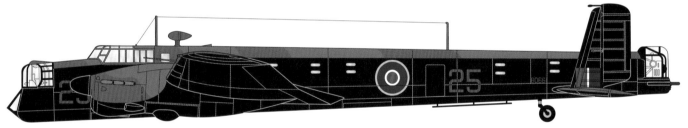

Armstrong Whitworth Whitley Mk.V BD661 '25'. Heavy Glider Conversion Unit, Brize Norton, Oxfordshire 1943
Unlike its brothers-in-arms, the Wellington and Hampden, the Whitley was designed from the very beginning to be a night bomber, a role it filled admirably in the first few years of the bombing campaign. Being replaced by the Lancaster and Halifax as a heavy bomber did not mean the end of useful service for the Whitley. Early marks had been operating with Coastal Command right from the outbreak of War; in 1942 Whitleys were used alongside Lysanders dropping agents into Occupied France; a bakers dozen were used by the BOAC as freighters supplying Malta; and it was from Whitleys that the paratroopers were dropped to take part in the famous Bruneval raid. Use as a glider tug was also a role that the Whitley was used in, '25' being used to tow Hotspur and Horsa gliders around Brize Norton to train the glider pilots for the coming invasion of Europe.
Reference used: p24 'Armstrong Whitworth Whitley' by Ken Wixey, Warpaint Series No. 21, Hall Park Books Ltd

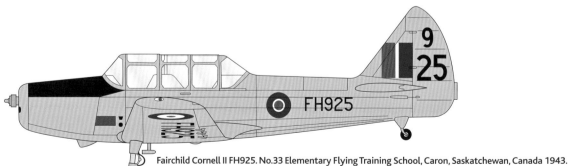

Fairchild Cornell II FH925. No.33 Elementary Flying Training School, Caron, Saskatchewan, Canada 1943.
The Fairchild PT-26 Cornell was a development of the PT-19, and was a request by the Royal Canadian Air Force for a dedicated elementary instrument trainer to replace the Tiger Moth and Fleet Finch aircraft, both biplanes, neither of which could afford the student pilots the grounding in instrument training that was necessary before they moved on to more modern types. Along with full instrumentation, the RCAF also specified that a fully enclosed canopy and adequate heating be fitted to keep out the often harsh winters that were prevalent in Canada. There were three distinct designations for the Cornell; the PT-26 was American built, exclusively for the RAF under the Lend-Lease agreement and known as the Cornell I; the PT-26A was built by Fleet in Canada and was the Cornell II, again for RAF use; and the PT-26B Cornell III was used by the Canadians.
Reference used: http://picasaweb.google.com/ih/photo/VX9fNUBusYmpMW1OxSNNoA

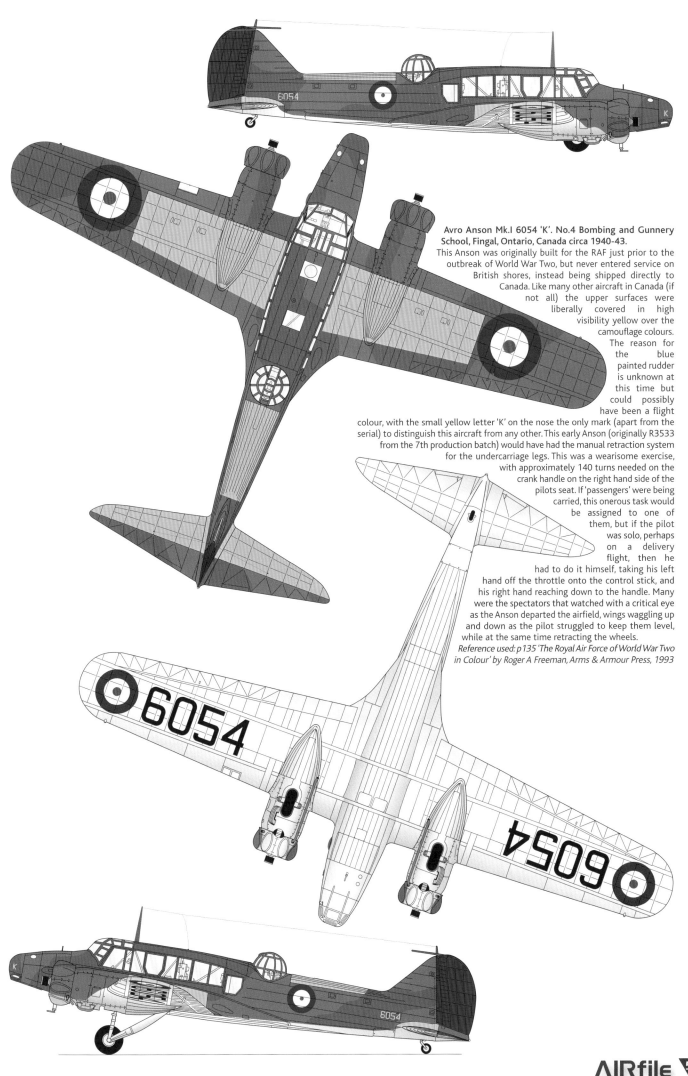

Avro Anson Mk.I 6054 'K'. No.4 Bombing and Gunnery School, Fingal, Ontario, Canada circa 1940-43.
This Anson was originally built for the RAF just prior to the outbreak of World War Two, but never entered service on British shores, instead being shipped directly to Canada. Like many other aircraft in Canada (if not all) the upper surfaces were liberally covered in high visibility yellow over the camouflage colours. The reason for the blue painted rudder is unknown at this time but could possibly have been a flight colour, with the small yellow letter 'K' on the nose the only mark (apart from the serial) to distinguish this aircraft from any other. This early Anson (originally R3533 from the 7th production batch) would have had the manual retraction system for the undercarriage legs. This was a wearisome exercise, with approximately 140 turns needed on the crank handle on the right hand side of the pilots seat. If 'passengers' were being carried, this onerous task would be assigned to one of them, but if the pilot was solo, perhaps on a delivery flight, then he had to do it himself, taking his left hand off the throttle onto the control stick, and his right hand reaching down to the handle. Many were the spectators that watched with a critical eye as the Anson departed the airfield, wings waggling up and down as the pilot struggled to keep them level, while at the same time retracting the wheels.
Reference used: p135 'The Royal Air Force of World War Two in Colour' by Roger A Freeman, Arms & Armour Press, 1993

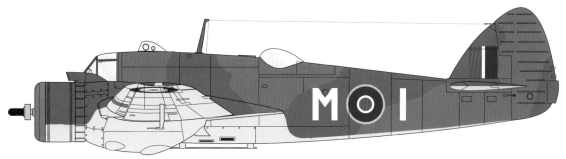

Bristol Beaufighter Mk.I 'M-1' (serial unknown). No.2 (Coastal) Operational Training Unit, RAF Catfoss, Yorkshire East Riding, 1943.
Formed in October 1940 at Catfoss, No.2 (Coastal) OTU was a training unit for twin-engined fighter and strike crews, many of these being deployed to Far East and Middle East squadrons. Initially Blenheims and Ansons were used, but from 1941 onwards, these were gradually replaced by Beaufighters and Beauforts. Designed initially as a twin-engined fighter, the Mk.1 Beaufighter was rather heavy and slow. Subsequently, its development for special duties like night fighting and long-range anti-shipping strikes allowed later marks to provide a valuable contribution to the war effort. By 1943 many Mk.1s would have been relegated to training duties.
Reference used: p20 RAF Flying Training and Support Units since 1912' by Ray Sturtivant with John Hamlin, Air-Britain (Historians) Ltd 2007

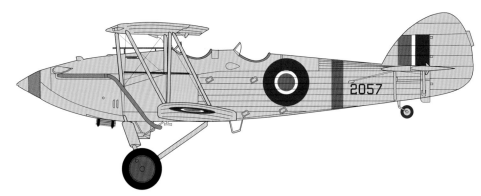

Hawker Hart Trainer 2057. No.23 Air School, Waterkloof Air Station, Pretoria, South Africa, circa 1943
The Hart Trainer was one of the first aircraft used in South Africa under the Joint Air Training Scheme. The initial batch of 100 Harts was purchased from the RAF for the nominal price of £200 each, proving excellent service and value until replaced by Masters and Harvards. While, initially, many trainee pilots grumbled at being allocated the old biplane Harts, they quickly revised their opinions once they had mastered the aircraft. Some Harts continued on until 1944 but became relegated to the early morning 'met climb' to gather information about the day's weather.
Reference used: p52 Yellow Wings: The Story of the Joint Air Training Scheme in World War 2' by Capt. Dave Becker, SAAF Museum Publications, 1989

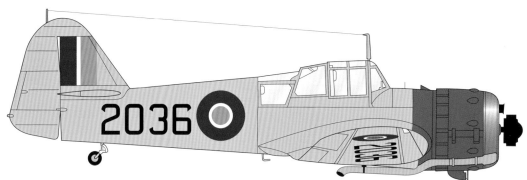

Miles Master II 2036. No.23 Air School, Waterkloof Air Station, Pretoria, South Africa, January 1943
Over 400 Miles Masters were shipped to South Africa and though its flying qualities made it a very good training aircraft, it suffered major technical problems while flying in the Dominion. The serviceability rate for Masters was a low as 20% throughout the year. This appeared to be due to lack of available spares and timber shrinkage that the airframe suffered from operating in the dry climate. Events came to a head in October 1943 when three Masters disintegrated in mid-air. Consequently, the SAAF refused point blank to use the Master as a trainer in their country. Most were replaced with Harvards, 240 of the remaining Masters were dismantled and returned to the UK. Fifty were retained and used for target towing.
Reference used: p136 'The Royal Air Force of World War Two in Colour' by Roger A Freeman, Arms & Armour Press, 1993

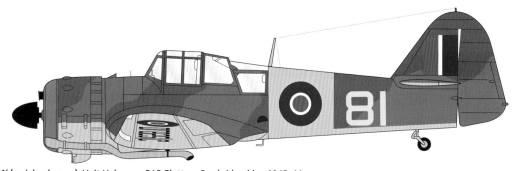

Miles Master II '81' (serial unknown). Unit Unknown, RAF Glatton, Cambridgeshire, 1943-44
RAF Glatton was used by the USAAF between 1943 and 1946, as the base of the 457th Bomb Group. During the months that the 457th Bomb Group was at Glatton, many aircraft landed at the field. Some landing for emergencies and others just visiting. Reference for this Miles Master II does not give any reasons why the aircraft landed at the base but it would have provided a colourful interlude for the USAAF airmen.
Reference used: http://www.457thbombgroup.org/Visitors/BBV.html

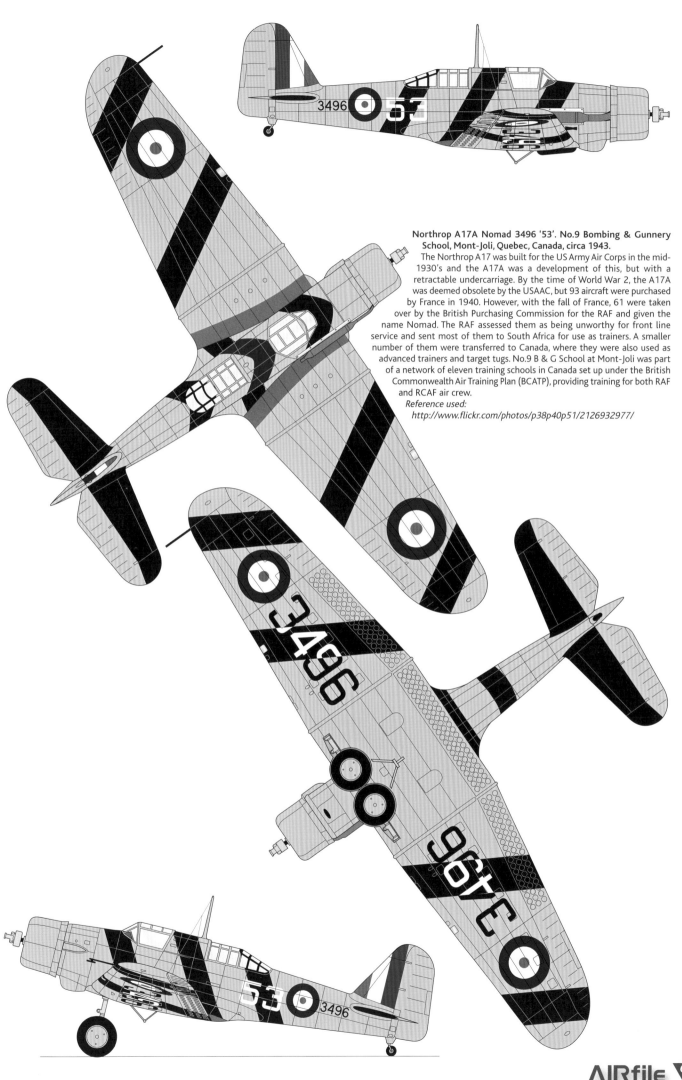

Northrop A17A Nomad 3496 '53'. No.9 Bombing & Gunnery School, Mont-Joli, Quebec, Canada, circa 1943.

The Northrop A17 was built for the US Army Air Corps in the mid-1930's and the A17A was a development of this, but with a retractable undercarriage. By the time of World War 2, the A17A was deemed obsolete by the USAAC, but 93 aircraft were purchased by France in 1940. However, with the fall of France, 61 were taken over by the British Purchasing Commission for the RAF and given the name Nomad. The RAF assessed them as being unworthy for front line service and sent most of them to South Africa for use as trainers. A smaller number of them were transferred to Canada, where they were also used as advanced trainers and target tugs. No.9 B & G School at Mont-Joli was part of a network of eleven training schools in Canada set up under the British Commonwealth Air Training Plan (BCATP), providing training for both RAF and RCAF air crew.

Reference used:
http://www.flickr.com/photos/p38p40p51/2126932977/

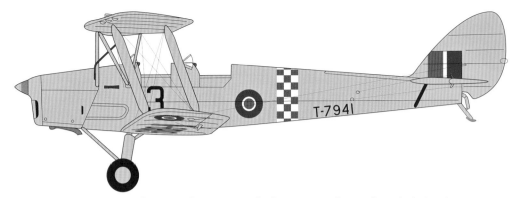

De Havilland DH82A Tiger Moth T-7941 '3'. No. 28 Elementary Flying Training School, Mount Hampden, Southern Rhodesia, February 1944
Mount Hampden was the home of No.28 EFTS from April 1941 through until the base was closed down in October 1945. The unit's motto, in the local Rhodesian dialect, was 'Pana Mazinana ano Bururuka' which translated was 'Here Fledglings take Wings'. The pupils of Mt Hampden had to share the same patch of sky as those at Belvedere, some 12 miles distant. So it was decided to give the Tiger Moths of Mt Hampden a distinguishing mark so that pupils transgressing flying orders in any way could be easily identified. At the time, the officer responsible for the logistics of training sorties was Flying Officer "Red" Danes, late of 56 Squadron, so he had the red and white chequerboard of his old squadron painted around the aft fuselage of each aircraft, which showed up very well against the all-yellow finish of all the training aircraft..
Reference used: p104 'RAF Flying Training and Support Units since 1912' by Ray Sturtivant with John Hamlin, Air-Britain (Historians) Ltd 2007

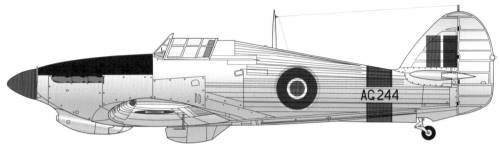

Hawker Hurricane Mk.X AG244. Central Flying School, Norton, Southern Rhodesia 1944.
Even before the Second World War had started, the steps for producing indigenous aircraft on foreign shores had already been taken, for the Canadian Car and Foundry Co. Ltd. had been awarded a contract to build Hurricanes in 1938. These aircraft started to be delivered at the beginning of 1940, as standard Mk.I Hurricanes. As licence built Merlin engines became available from the Packard company, these aircraft were re-designated Mk.X. Very few of this particular Mark flew with the RAF, as most of the second batch from which AG244 came were sent to Russia, so to be flying in Southern Rhodesia makes this Hurricane a fairly rare bird.
Reference used: from the collection of Mike Starmer

Miles Magister Mk.I L6907 'TBR-K'. Staff College Flight, Technical Training Command, White Waltham 1944
Up to the outbreak of War in 1939, the Staff College trained Officers for duties in the Air Ministry, Command Centres and various Headquarters within the RAF. Temporarily closed down on the day the War started, the College resumed in late 1939. L6907 was probably used as a hack and runabout aircraft for the Officers and shows late War markings, the roundels now being 'National Marking No.2' (more popularly known as 'C' type), revised fin flash, yellow fuselage band and white code letters. The significance of the bird motif is unknown. This aircraft survived the War, but only until 1948, crashing at Hammerwood on the 19th of July of that year.
Reference used: p6 'Miles Magister' by Michael Ovcacik & Karel Susa, 4+ Publication, Mark 1 Ltd, 2001

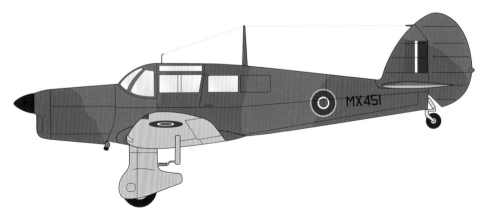

Percival Proctor Mk.IV MX451, No.1 Radio School, Cranwell, Lincolnshire, circa 1944
While the Proctor Mk.I was a dedicated communications aircraft, the Mk.II and Mk.III were equipped as radio trainers. The last version, the Mk.IV, was also a radio trainer, but was bigger than the II and III and carried radio equipment that the trainee would actually be using when sent to an operational Squadron. The training and service these aircraft gave is little known and largely un-heralded, considering that the Proctors numbered over 760 in service with the RAF, and some continued to serve as communication aircraft into 1955. The large number built meant that surplus aircraft were sold to the civilian market Post-War.
Reference used: p456 'Aircraft of the Royal Air Force since 1918' by Owen Thetford, Guild Publishing London 1988

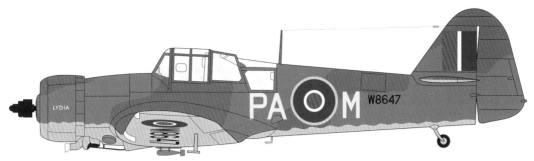

Miles Master III W8647 'PA-M' 'LYDIA'. No.3 Tactical Exercise Unit, Aston Down, Gloucestershire, late 1944.
Nose art in the RAF during Wartime was not exactly prolific, so for a Miles Master to carry a name on the cowling is highly unusual and rare. 'Lydia' was used to train Typhoon pilots in the art of ground attack, carrying light practise bombs on a belly mounted rack, so possibly the naming of the aircraft was down to the influence of the fighter boys. The demarcation between the upper camouflage colours and the yellow undersides is also unusual, as a rarely seen scalloped edge, and the fighter style Sky squadron codes were generally not seen on Wartime Masters.
Reference used: p374 Miles Military Trainers' by Alan W Hall, Scale Military Modelling, Volume 19 Number 8 October 1997, Guidelines Publications 1997

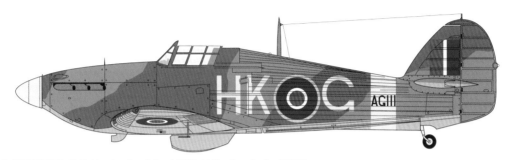

Hawker Hurricane Mk.X AG111 'HK-G'. Fighter Leaders School, Milfield, Northumberland 1944
The move of the Fighter Leaders School to Milfield in early 1944, coincided with the build up plans for the invasion of Europe. The courses that Flight Leaders and Squadron Leaders did at the School trained them in the tactical requirements of the invasion and advance from the bridgehead, how to operate their squadrons from primitive airstrips in close support of the ground troops and in the planned rapid movement through France, sometimes from airfields the Germans had recently left.
Reference used: from the collection of Mike Starmer

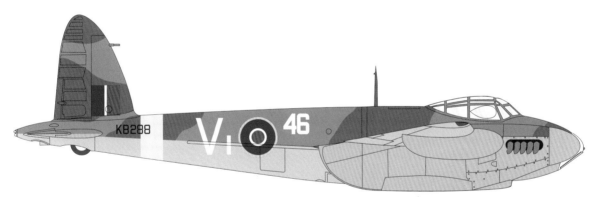

De Havilland Mosquito B.20 KB288 'V1-46'. No.31 Operational Training Unit, Debert, Nova Scotia, Canada, October 1944
Established at Debert, Nova Scotia in May 1941, No.31 OTU was tasked with training general reconnaissance crews. Due to increased U-boat activity in the Western Atlantic, the unit flew operational patrols from Dartmouth, Nova Scotia during 1942. Originally flying Ansons and Hudsons, Mosquitos began to arrive for the unit in May 1944. KB288 suffered undercarriage failure in October 1944 and was struck off charge in November of the same year due to further mishaps.
Reference used: from the collection of Mike Starmer

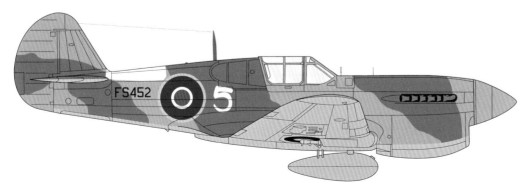

Curtiss Kittyhawk II FS452 '5', No. 239 Wing Training Flight, Cervia, Italy 1944-45
The serial code of this Kittyhawk II, FS452, shows that it was the equivalent of a USAAF P-40L, and one of approximately 100 supplied to the RAF and used in the Mediterranean area. The Mk.II designation also covered the P-40F, which was externally similar. The L version was an attempt by Curtiss to bring down the operating weight of the P-40F, by removing two of the guns, and reducing the armour plating, fuel and ammunition. There are certain aspects of FS452 that are of note. The lack of tail flash is unusual, and the reference photograph shows no under wing roundels, possibly due to an over-painting of trainer yellow. No Squadron codes are used, simply a roughly applied '5' in white. The canopy also has white applied on the upper side, perhaps a vain attempt to ward off the Mediterranean sun. The light patch forward of the tail could be either white or yellow, for reasons unknown.
Reference used: p294 RAF Flying Training and Support Units since 1912' by Ray Sturtivant with John Hamlin, Air-Britain (Historians) Ltd 2007

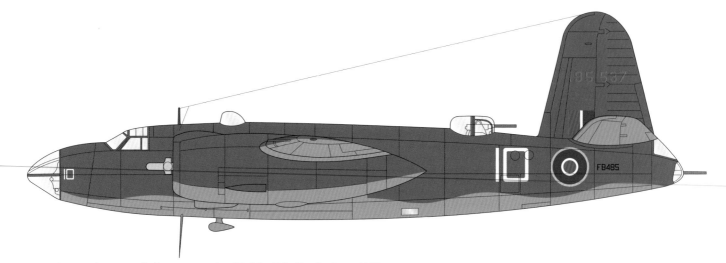

Martin Marauder II FB485 '10' No.70 Operational Training Unit, Shandur, Egypt 1944.
7 OTU was formed at Ismailia in Egypt in December 1940. Its task was to train pilots to operate in Middle Eastern conditions and as such was equipped to train twin-engined crews, single seat fighter pilots and crews for communications duties. After a short period of service at Nakuru, Kenya, in May 1943 it began moving to Shandur, but this was not completed until August. At this time Marauders replaced the Blenheims and it continued in its training role until disbanding on 16 July 1945. Note FB485's over-painted US serials on the fin.
Reference used: p207 RAF Flying Training and Support Units since 1912' by Ray Sturtivant with John Hamlin, Air-Britain (Historians) Ltd 2007

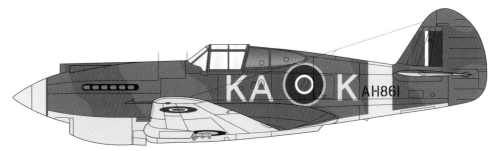

Curtiss Tomahawk I AH861 'KA-K' No.82 Operational Training Unit, Ossington, Nottinghamshire 1944
The P-40 series of aircraft was used on practically every front during World War II, from Alaska to the Pacific, from Europe to Africa and all points in between. Despite the vast numbers used by nearly all the Allies, only two countries actually bought the aircraft, the United States and Britain. France was originally going to be the initial purchaser of the export version, the Model 81, but for obvious reasons, these could not be delivered. The 140 aircraft of the French order were bought by the British and given the name Tomahawk I. AH861 was part of this order. These aircraft were quickly deemed to be unsuitable for combat and were relegated to training duties. No. 82 OTU trained night bomber crews, using Wellingtons, and AH861 was on strength as one of the support aircraft.
Reference used: p207 RAF Flying Training and Support Units since 1912' by Ray Sturtivant with John Hamlin, Air-Britain (Historians) Ltd 2007

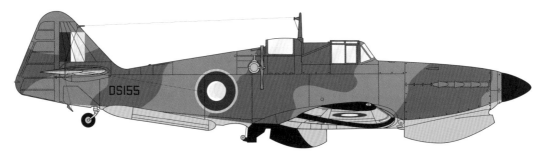

Boulton Paul Defiant TT Mk.I DS155. 'A' Flight, No.22 Anti-Aircraft Co-operation Unit, Poona, India 1944-45.
Pilot: Sqn. Ldr. W Young
There was a great need for target tug aircraft, both at home and abroad, and this was the main reason that the Defiant was given a second lease of life. Overseas, Defiant aircraft were easily recognised by the tropical filter under the nose. Another giveaway on this particular aircraft is the hasty over-painting of the red in the roundel. With only the serial number showing, an otherwise anonymous DS155 was one of 54 Defiants used by 22 AACU on the Indian Continent, the greatest amount used by any of the AAC Units. This Unit was to become an Indian Air Force Unit from its inception in March of 1943 until disbandment in October of 1946. DS155 was one of the last TT Defiants flying, only being struck off charge on the 1st of January 1947.
Reference used: p20 'Boulton Paul Defiant' by Alan W Hall, Warpaint Series No. 42, Warpaint Books Ltd

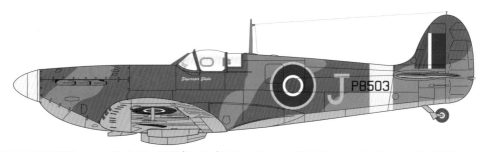

Supermarine Spitfire Mk.IIa P8503 'J' 'Skyscraper Sheila'. No.1690 (Bomber) Defence Training Flight, Syerston, Nottinghamshire 1945
Spitfire P8503 had a very active life from the moment it went to its first squadron until the point where it joined the BDFU, having been with six squadrons and the Air Fighting Development Unit. Retired from frontline service, P8503 was used by the BDFU to train bomber crews how to defend themselves against fighter attacks. Each Bomber Group had several flights like this and their role at this point in the War was more and more relevant as Bomber Command was making ever more incursions into Germany during daylight hours. The BDFU disbanded in 1945.
Reference used: from the collection of Mike Starmer

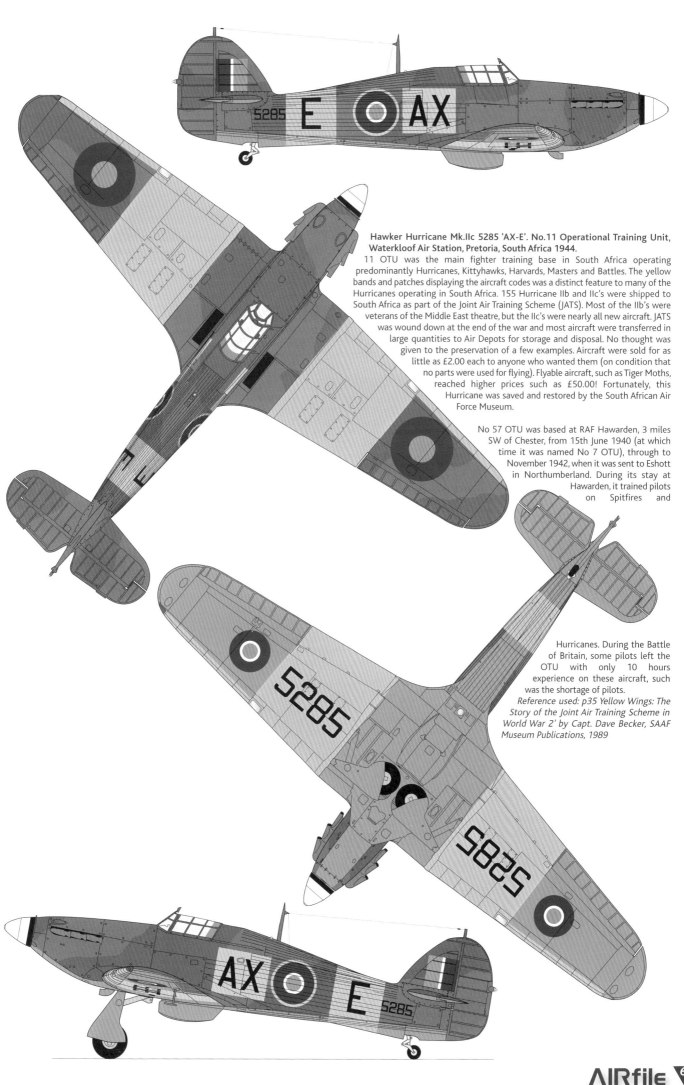

Hawker Hurricane Mk.IIc 5285 'AX-E'. No.11 Operational Training Unit, Waterkloof Air Station, Pretoria, South Africa 1944.

11 OTU was the main fighter training base in South Africa operating predominantly Hurricanes, Kittyhawks, Harvards, Masters and Battles. The yellow bands and patches displaying the aircraft codes was a distinct feature to many of the Hurricanes operating in South Africa. 155 Hurricane IIb and IIc's were shipped to South Africa as part of the Joint Air Training Scheme (JATS). Most of the IIb's were veterans of the Middle East theatre, but the IIc's were nearly all new aircraft. JATS was wound down at the end of the war and most aircraft were transferred in large quantities to Air Depots for storage and disposal. No thought was given to the preservation of a few examples. Aircraft were sold for as little as £2.00 each to anyone who wanted them (on condition that no parts were used for flying). Flyable aircraft, such as Tiger Moths, reached higher prices such as £50.00! Fortunately, this Hurricane was saved and restored by the South African Air Force Museum.

No 57 OTU was based at RAF Hawarden, 3 miles SW of Chester, from 15th June 1940 (at which time it was named No 7 OTU), through to November 1942, when it was sent to Eshott in Northumberland. During its stay at Hawarden, it trained pilots on Spitfires and Hurricanes. During the Battle of Britain, some pilots left the OTU with only 10 hours experience on these aircraft, such was the shortage of pilots.

Reference used: p35 Yellow Wings: The Story of the Joint Air Training Scheme in World War 2' by Capt. Dave Becker, SAAF Museum Publications, 1989

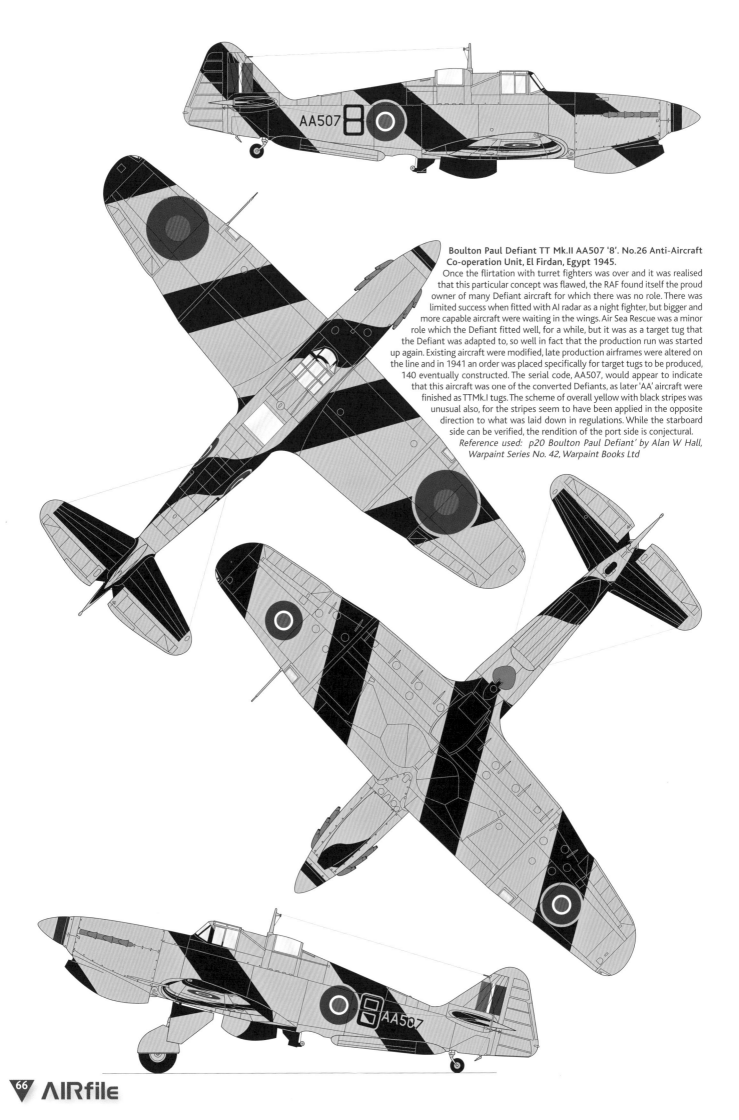

Boulton Paul Defiant TT Mk.II AA507 '8'. No.26 Anti-Aircraft Co-operation Unit, El Firdan, Egypt 1945.

Once the flirtation with turret fighters was over and it was realised that this particular concept was flawed, the RAF found itself the proud owner of many Defiant aircraft for which there was no role. There was limited success when fitted with AI radar as a night fighter, but bigger and more capable aircraft were waiting in the wings. Air Sea Rescue was a minor role which the Defiant fitted well, for a while, but it was as a target tug that the Defiant was adapted to, so well in fact that the production run was started up again. Existing aircraft were modified, late production airframes were altered on the line and in 1941 an order was placed specifically for target tugs to be produced, 140 eventually constructed. The serial code, AA507, would appear to indicate that this aircraft was one of the converted Defiants, as later 'AA' aircraft were finished as TTMk.I tugs. The scheme of overall yellow with black stripes was unusual also, for the stripes seem to have been applied in the opposite direction to what was laid down in regulations. While the starboard side can be verified, the rendition of the port side is conjectural.

Reference used: p20 Boulton Paul Defiant' by Alan W Hall, Warpaint Series No. 42, Warpaint Books Ltd

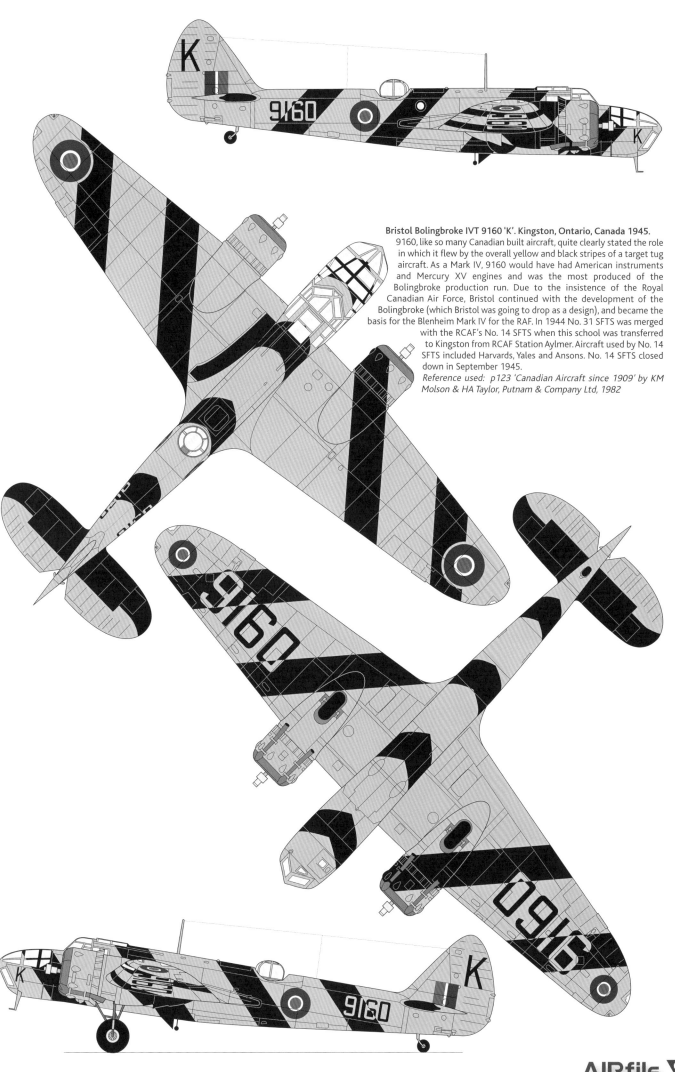

Bristol Bolingbroke IVT 9160 'K'. Kingston, Ontario, Canada 1945.
9160, like so many Canadian built aircraft, quite clearly stated the role in which it flew by the overall yellow and black stripes of a target tug aircraft. As a Mark IV, 9160 would have had American instruments and Mercury XV engines and was the most produced of the Bolingbroke production run. Due to the insistence of the Royal Canadian Air Force, Bristol continued with the development of the Bolingbroke (which Bristol was going to drop as a design), and became the basis for the Blenheim Mark IV for the RAF. In 1944 No. 31 SFTS was merged with the RCAF's No. 14 SFTS when this school was transferred to Kingston from RCAF Station Aylmer. Aircraft used by No. 14 SFTS included Harvards, Yales and Ansons. No. 14 SFTS closed down in September 1945.
Reference used: p123 'Canadian Aircraft since 1909' by KM Molson & HA Taylor, Putnam & Company Ltd, 1982

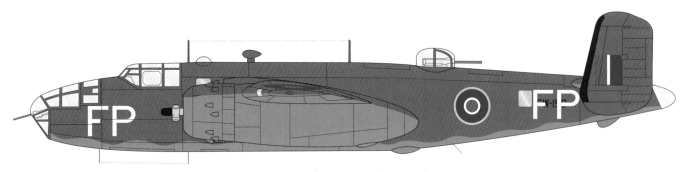

North American Mitchell II FW150 'FP'. No.111 Operational Training Squadron, Nassau, Bahamas, early 1945
The B-25 Mitchell was a classic, twin-engined bomber of World War II, and will be forever remembered in history as the aircraft that took the fight back to the enemy in the shape of the Royce Raids and the Doolittle Raid in April of 1942. Almost 11,000 Mitchell aircraft were built, and served admirably on all fronts. The RAF made use of over 800 Mitchells over the European and Mediterranean theatres, with the Mark II version the most prolific in number. FW150 was not only used to train RAF aircrews on American aircraft, it also took part in anti-submarine patrols alongside the local American units of the Air Force and Navy.
Reference used: p207 RAF Flying Training and Support Units since 1912' by Ray Sturtivant with John Hamlin, Air-Britain (Historians) Ltd 2007

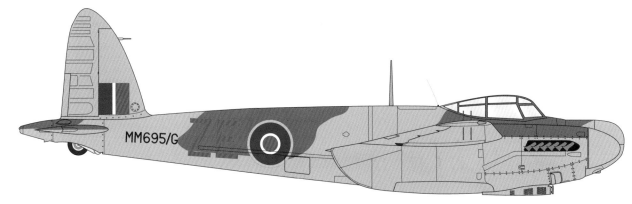

De Havilland Mosquito NF.30 MM695/G 'ZL'. Central Fighter Establishment, RAF Tangmere, Sussex 1945.
The forward profile of the Mosquito was drastically altered by the fitting of the two stage Merlin engines and the 'Bullnose' housing over the Airborne Interception Mk.X radar. This was the British designation for the American built SCR 720/729 radar, an instrument that would also equip the P-61 Black Widow, an aircraft that had been designed from the outset to be a night fighter, something that the other combatants never had, having to alter existing airframes. Indeed, the RAF did not have a dedicated night fighter until after the War. Mosquito MM695 carried the 'G' suffix to indicate that it should be under armed guard while on the ground, and while the 'ZE' code of the CFE was present, an individual aircraft letter was not.
Reference used: p59 'De Havilland Mosquito - An Illustrated History' by Stuart Howe, Crecy Publishing Limited 1999

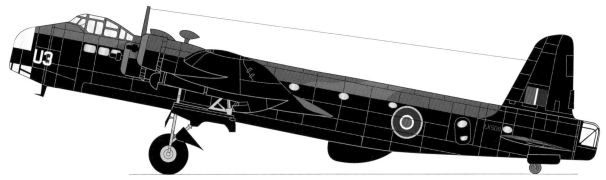

Short Stirling Mk.IV LK508 'U3'. Empire Air Navigation School, Shawbury, Shropshire 1945
Stirling LK508 was one of only two used by the Empire Air Navigation School and during the time spent with them it made at least one transatlantic flight. Starting life as a Mk. III, one of 429 built by Austin Motors Limited at Longbridge, LK508 was one of 37 later converted to Mk. IV standard. This involved the removal of all armament, including front and upper turrets and adding a U-shaped metal bar under the gunless rear turret for the towing of gliders. Mk. IV Stirlings were also heavily used for Special Operations and for parachute drops. Stirlings of various marks were given a second lease of life when they were used extensively as glider tugs for the imminent invasion of Europe.
Reference used: p22 'Short Stirling' by Alan W Hall, Warpaint Series No. 15

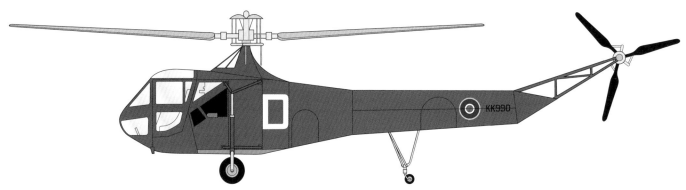

Sikorsky R-4B Hoverfly I KK990. Helicopter Training Flight, No.43 Operational Training Unit, Andover, Hampshire 1945-46.
While other countries had dabbled with the helicopter idea, it was America and Igor Sikorsky that led the way with the first practicable helicopter, the R-4, from January 1942. Although seriously under-powered and slow, the potential of machines like this were already being recognised and would go on to be an important part of future aviation. Named the Hoverfly I by the RAF, trials started with the aircraft at No. 43 OTU at Andover in February 1945. By April of 1945, the Helicopter Training Flight was a separate unit, and was set up to convert Air Observation Pilots. The Flight did not last long and was dis-banded in January 1946. KK990 was one of 45 machines that were supplied to Britain.
Reference used: www.flightglobal.com & www.airliners.net

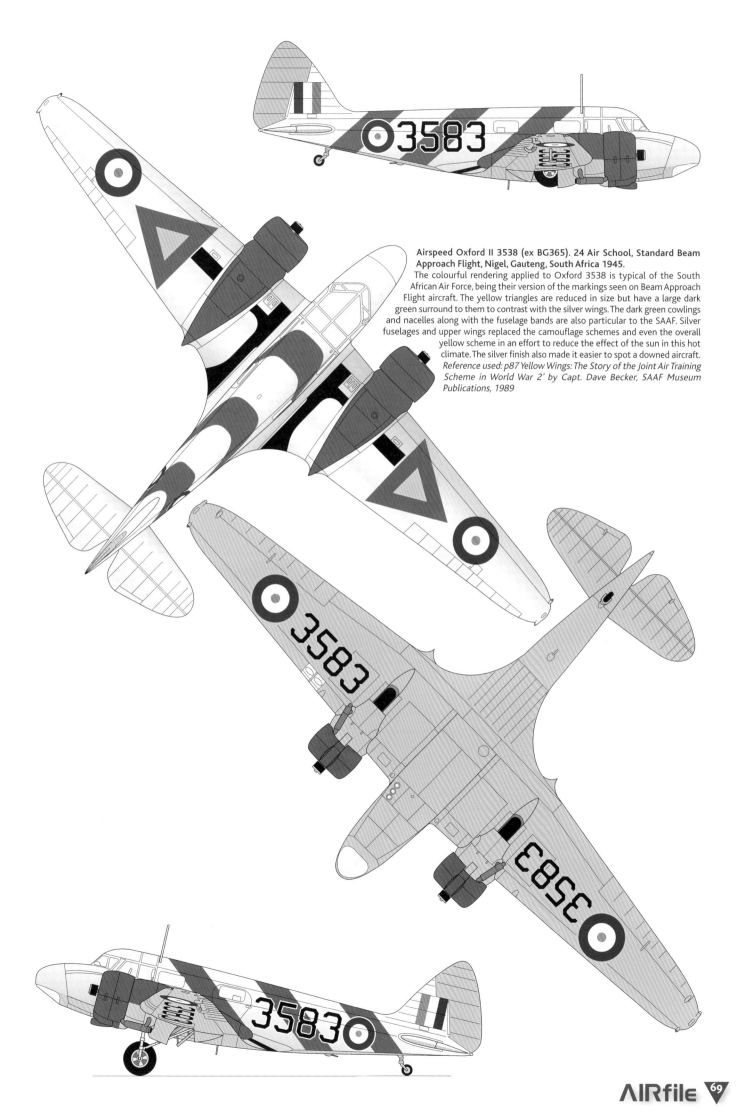

Airspeed Oxford II 3538 (ex BG365). 24 Air School, Standard Beam Approach Flight, Nigel, Gauteng, South Africa 1945.

The colourful rendering applied to Oxford 3538 is typical of the South African Air Force, being their version of the markings seen on Beam Approach Flight aircraft. The yellow triangles are reduced in size but have a large dark green surround to them to contrast with the silver wings. The dark green cowlings and nacelles along with the fuselage bands are also particular to the SAAF. Silver fuselages and upper wings replaced the camouflage schemes and even the overall yellow scheme in an effort to reduce the effect of the sun in this hot climate. The silver finish also made it easier to spot a downed aircraft.
Reference used: p87 Yellow Wings: The Story of the Joint Air Training Scheme in World War 2' by Capt. Dave Becker, SAAF Museum Publications, 1989

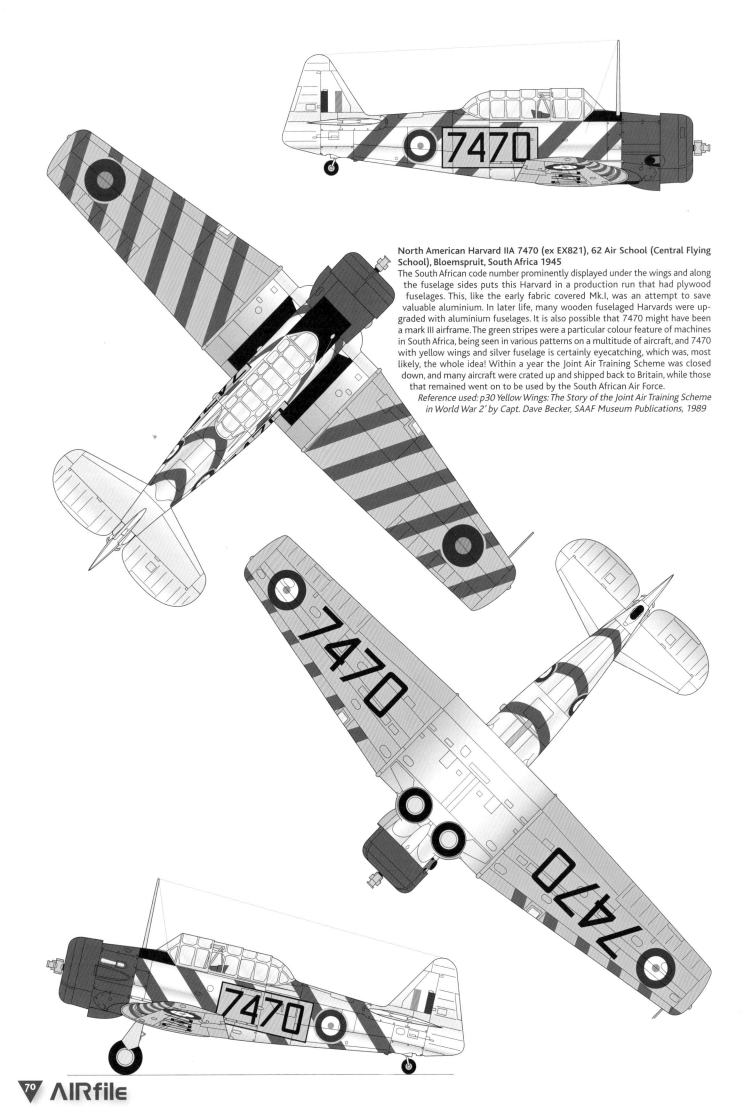

North American Harvard IIA 7470 (ex EX821), 62 Air School (Central Flying School), Bloemspruit, South Africa 1945

The South African code number prominently displayed under the wings and along the fuselage sides puts this Harvard in a production run that had plywood fuselages. This, like the early fabric covered Mk.I, was an attempt to save valuable aluminium. In later life, many wooden fuselaged Harvards were upgraded with aluminium fuselages. It is also possible that 7470 might have been a mark III airframe. The green stripes were a particular colour feature of machines in South Africa, being seen in various patterns on a multitude of aircraft, and 7470 with yellow wings and silver fuselage is certainly eyecatching, which was, most likely, the whole idea! Within a year the Joint Air Training Scheme was closed down, and many aircraft were crated up and shipped back to Britain, while those that remained went on to be used by the South African Air Force.

Reference used: p30 Yellow Wings: The Story of the Joint Air Training Scheme in World War 2' by Capt. Dave Becker, SAAF Museum Publications, 1989

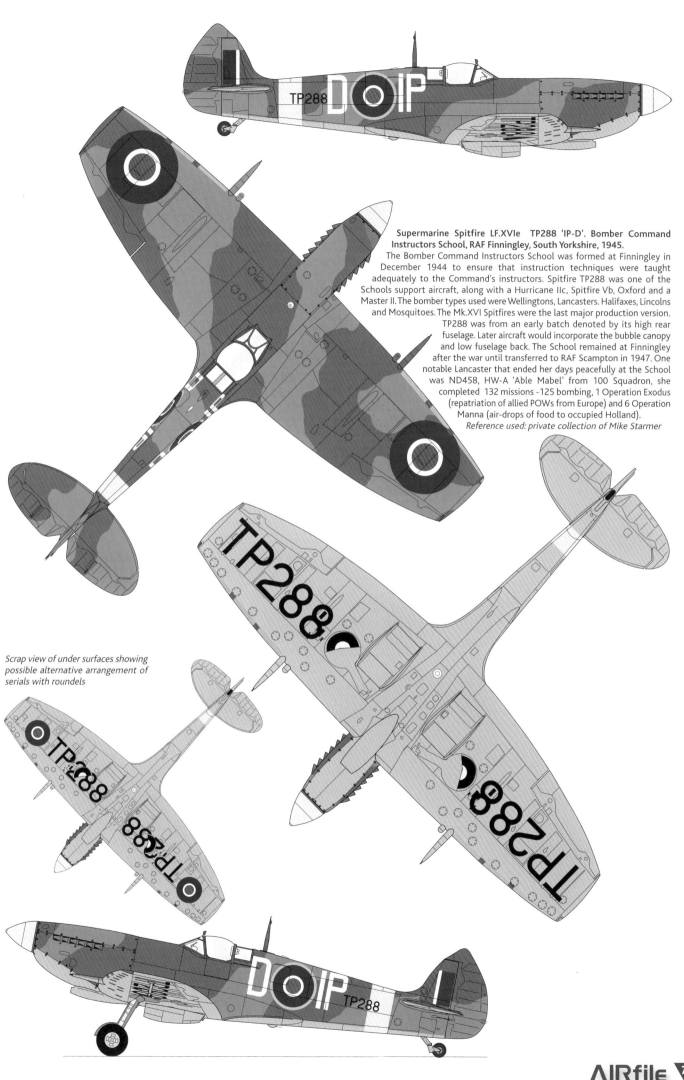

Supermarine Spitfire LF.XVIe TP288 'IP-D'. Bomber Command Instructors School, RAF Finningley, South Yorkshire, 1945.

The Bomber Command Instructors School was formed at Finningley in December 1944 to ensure that instruction techniques were taught adequately to the Command's instructors. Spitfire TP288 was one of the Schools support aircraft, along with a Hurricane IIc, Spitfire Vb, Oxford and a Master II. The bomber types used were Wellingtons, Lancasters. Halifaxes, Lincolns and Mosquitoes. The Mk.XVI Spitfires were the last major production version. TP288 was from an early batch denoted by its high rear fuselage. Later aircraft would incorporate the bubble canopy and low fuselage back. The School remained at Finningley after the war until transferred to RAF Scampton in 1947. One notable Lancaster that ended her days peacefully at the School was ND458, HW-A 'Able Mabel' from 100 Squadron, she completed 132 missions -125 bombing, 1 Operation Exodus (repatriation of allied POWs from Europe) and 6 Operation Manna (air-drops of food to occupied Holland).

Reference used: private collection of Mike Starmer

Scrap view of under surfaces showing possible alternative arrangement of serials with roundels

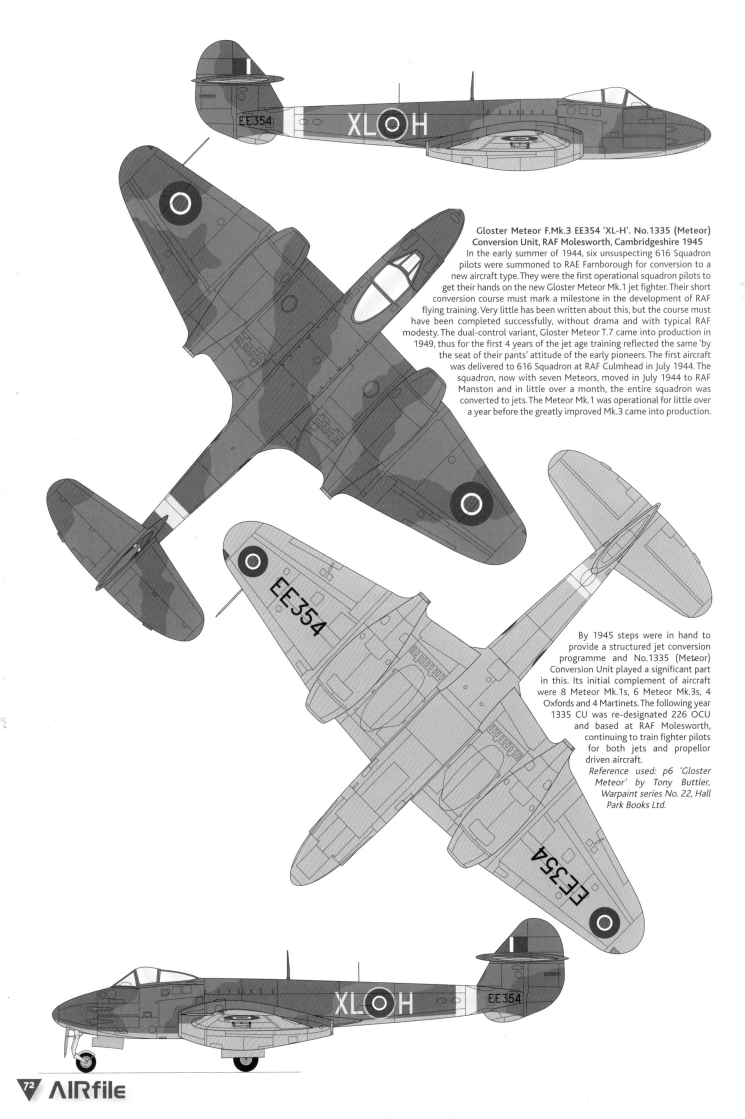

Gloster Meteor F.Mk.3 EE354 'XL-H'. No.1335 (Meteor) Conversion Unit, RAF Molesworth, Cambridgeshire 1945

In the early summer of 1944, six unsuspecting 616 Squadron pilots were summoned to RAE Farnborough for conversion to a new aircraft type. They were the first operational squadron pilots to get their hands on the new Gloster Meteor Mk.1 jet fighter. Their short conversion course must mark a milestone in the development of RAF flying training. Very little has been written about this, but the course must have been completed successfully, without drama and with typical RAF modesty. The dual-control variant, Gloster Meteor T.7 came into production in 1949, thus for the first 4 years of the jet age training reflected the same 'by the seat of their pants' attitude of the early pioneers. The first aircraft was delivered to 616 Squadron at RAF Culmhead in July 1944. The squadron, now with seven Meteors, moved in July 1944 to RAF Manston and in little over a month, the entire squadron was converted to jets. The Meteor Mk.1 was operational for little over a year before the greatly improved Mk.3 came into production.

By 1945 steps were in hand to provide a structured jet conversion programme and No.1335 (Meteor) Conversion Unit played a significant part in this. Its initial complement of aircraft were 8 Meteor Mk.1s, 6 Meteor Mk.3s, 4 Oxfords and 4 Martinets. The following year 1335 CU was re-designated 226 OCU and based at RAF Molesworth, continuing to train fighter pilots for both jets and propellor driven aircraft.

Reference used: p6 'Gloster Meteor' by Tony Buttler, Warpaint series No. 22, Hall Park Books Ltd.